The Journey from Heartache to Hope

40 Devotionals to Help You on Your Way

**Alane Pearce &
Laura Savage-Rains**

Three Circle Press

The Journey from Heartache to Hope:
40 Devotionals to Help You On Your Way
by Alane Pearce and Laura Savage-Rains
© 2022 by Alane Pearce and Laura Savage-Rains

ISBN: 978-1-7333166-3-7

All rights reserved. No part of this publication may be reproduced, stored in a retrieval system, or transmitted in any form or by any means—for example, electronic, photocopy, recording—without the prior written permission of the author. The only exception is brief quotations in printed reviews.

Published by Three Circle Press
114 World of Tennis Sq., Lakeway, Texas 78738

Printed in the United States of America First Printing 2022

Paperbook design and eBook design by Pearce Writing Services
Cover design by Three Circle Press, cover image public domain from WikiMedia.org
Claude Monet - Water Lilies and Japanese Bridge - y1972-15 - Princeton University Art Museum.jpg

Scripture quotations marked CEB are taken from the *Common English Bible*, copyright 2011. Used by permission. All rights reserved.

Scripture quotations marked TLB are taken from *The Living Bible* copyright © 1971 by Tyndale House Foundation. Used by permission of Tyndale House Publishers Inc., Carol Stream, Illinois 60188. All rights reserved. The Living Bible, TLB, and the The Living Bible logo are registered trademarks of Tyndale House Publishers.

Scripture quotations marked MSG are taken from *THE MESSAGE*, copyright © 1993, 2002, 2018 by Eugene H. Peterson. Used by permission of NavPress. All rights reserved. Represented by Tyndale House Publishers, Inc.

Scripture quotations marked NIV is taken from *THE HOLY BIBLE, NEW INTERNATIONAL VERSION*®, NIV® Copyright © 1973, 1978, 1984, 2011 by Biblica, Inc.® Used by permission. All rights reserved worldwide. "New International Version" and "NIV" are registered trademarks of Biblica, Inc.®. Used with permission.

Scripture quotations marked NLT are taken from the *Holy Bible, New Living Translation*, copyright © 1996, 2004, 2015 by Tyndale House Foundation. Used by permission of Tyndale House Publishers, Inc., Carol Stream, Illinois 60188. All rights reserved.

Scripture quotations marked NRSVUE are taken from the *New Revised Standard Version Updated Edition*. Copyright © 2021 National Council of Churches of Christ in the United States of America. Used by permission. All rights reserved worldwide.

Scripture quotations marked AMP are taken from the *Amplified Bible*, Copyright © 2015 by The Lockman Foundation, La Habra, CA 90631. All rights reserved.

For God alone my soul waits in silence;
   from him comes my salvation.
He alone is my rock and my salvation,
   my fortress; I shall never be shaken.

For God alone my soul waits in silence,
   for my hope is from him.
He alone is my rock and my salvation,
   my fortress; I shall not be shaken.
On God rests my deliverance and my
   honor; my mighty rock, my refuge is in God.

Trust in him at all times, O people;
   pour out your heart before him;
   God is a refuge for us.

Selah

Psalm 62:1-2, 5-8 NRSVUE

"This uplifting devotional offers insight from real people in the Bible who found a reason to hope even in the midst of their struggles. When you read about them, you will be encouraged to know you are not alone. For me, this is a valuable reminder that hope can truly be found even when life is hard."

Susan Campbell, Author
More Than You Imagine Ministries
A Wild & Wonderful Life,
Do You Like Peas?

"Alane and Laura remind us that no heartache is too hard for God. Their adept reading of the Scriptures and their beautiful writing compel us into God's heart. We see ourselves in the women and men of the Scriptures who opened themselves to God in their most vulnerable circumstances. In pointing us to hear, open, prepare and embrace, these wise writers prepare our generation for enduring the heartaches of our times with the eternal hope of the Lord."

Rev. Denise Nance Pierce, Associate Minister
Greater Mt. Zion Baptist Church
and Attorney at Law

Table of Contents

*Authors listed as AP for Alane Pearce
and LSR for Laura Savage-Rains*

A Note from the Authors	7
Prologue	
The Rich Young Ruler Turned Away from Hope [AP]	11

HEAR   15

Hagar Heard God's Voice in Her Loneliness [LSR]	17
Jacob Heard Directly from God [AP]	21
Deborah Heard God's Voice as She Faced the Enemy [LSR]	25
Samuel Heard a Disappointing Message from God [LSR]	29
Haggai Heard God's Correction [AP]	33
Zechariah Heard a Special-Delivery Answer to Prayer [LSR]	37
Mary Sat at Jesus' Feet to Hear His Words [AP]	41
Paul Heard God Say "No"—Multiple Times! [LSR]	45

OPEN   49

Esau Was Open to Forgiving after a Deep Betrayal [AP]	51
Joshua Was Open to God's Power to Prevail [LSR]	55
Naomi Was Open to Help [AP]	59
Nehemiah Opened Himself to Ridicule to Show God's Power [LSR]	63
Elizabeth Opened Her Life to Someone Else's Joy [LSR]	67
Jairus Was Open to Having Faith [AP]	71
A Woman Caught in Adultery Was Open to Jesus' Compassion [AP]	75
The Man Born Blind Was Open to God's Purpose [AP]	79
Mary Magdalene Opened Herself to a New Reality [LSR]	83
Lydia Opened Her Home at the Risk of Her Livelihood [LSR]	87

PREPARE   91

Miriam Prepared to Lead Others in Worship [LSR]	93
Joseph Was Prepared for Leadership Through Trials [LSR]	97
Ruth Prepared to Help [AP]	101

David Prepared His Heart [AP]	105
Huldah Prepared to Speak the Difficult Truth from God's Word [LSR]	109
Anna Prepared to See the Long-Awaited Savior by Worshiping Daily [LSR]	113
The Samaritan Woman Was Prepared to Discuss Deeply Troubling Questions [LSR]	117
The Sick Woman Prepared for Healing [AP]	121

EMBRACE   125

Eve Embraced the Possibilities That More Children Could Bring [LSR]	127
Leah Embraced a God-First Attitude [AP]	131
Hannah Embraced the Power of Prayer and Prophecy [LSR]	135
Esther Embraced God's Purpose for Her Position [AP]	139
Hosea Embraced God's Redemption [AP]	143
Habakkuk Embraced Joy Despite Challenging Circumstances [AP]	147
Mary Embraced the Disgrace that Came with Following God's Will [LSR]	151
John The Baptist Embraced Jesus as Messiah [AP]	155
Martha Embraced the Power of Jesus' Resurrection [LSR]	159
The Poor Widow Embraced Faith [AP]	163
Peter Embraced Jesus' Forgiveness [AP]	167
John Mark Experienced Failure and Then Embraced Reconciliation [LSR]	171
Timothy Embraced His Calling [AP]	175

About Heartache to Hope Retreat	179
About Alane Pearce	180
About Laura Savage-Rains	181
List of Heartaches	183
List of Hopes	185
SUBJECT INDEX	187
SCRIPTURE INDEX	194
Acknowledgments	196

A Note from the Authors

We have each learned that heartache comes to us in all forms. The death of a loved-one is one form. There are many others. Heartaches can come when we feel alone, struggle with hard questions, find ourselves in a situation we didn't want to be in, or face criticism for what we believe. Our hearts can ache for a loved-one's bad decisions, or when we experience big changes. What we've learned in our personal struggles is that God is always there with us, right in the middle of the pain. He hears our cries and he understands our suffering. He also wants us to find hope in the midst of our heartaches.

Alane Pearce is an author, teacher, and encourager of women. Her experiences with infertility, miscarriages, and the death of her 15-day-old son led her to a crisis of faith where she had to decide why she followed God. Was it because of what he did or didn't do for her, or because of what he had already done for her through salvation in Jesus?

As she wrestled with God in her pain and grief, Alane began to understand God's love, healing, and compassion in a very personal way. As a result, she learned first-hand how much comfort and compassion God gives those who are struggling and hurting.

She now devotes her ministry to helping women understand the deep, abiding, and everlasting love God has for his children. Through speaking, writing, and coaching, Alane's story inspires and encourages women around the globe.

Laura Savage-Rains loves to teach—especially about the lesser known stories of women in the Bible. She currently teaches a women's Bible study in the church where her musician husband, Mark, leads the traditional worship service. Over the years, Laura has taught in universities and seminaries in four countries and has led women's conferences and retreats throughout the US.

As an only child, Laura grew to treasure deep, one-on-one friendships. She constantly dreamed of one day having a husband, but marriage did not come until she was 46 years old. The heartaches of those single years included numerous broken hearts, the painful longing for a soul mate, and the unhappy realization that the hopes of becoming a mother were passing her by. While she shared the joy of her girlfriends who found husbands and relished becoming "auntie" to her friends' children, the desire for a family of her own never waned.

Thankfully, Laura grew up in a youth group where she was taught to study the Scriptures daily and to rely on Christ's strength. She learned that Jesus was truly the only husband she *needed*, yet wanting a human one never left her heart. As many a dateless weekend turned into decades of singleness, Laura stayed faithful to the study of Scripture and discovered the profound truths that empowered her to live an abundant, joy-filled life even as a single adult.

Because we both have experienced our measure of heartache—from losing loved ones, to childlessness, to longing for marriage into mid-life, dealing with health issues, and caring for aging and sickly parents—we know how hard life can be sometimes. We both also know that when we reach out to God in times of heartache, he is always there for us.

As we looked at Scripture to understand how God views our heartaches and griefs, we saw that the people of the Bible also had trials and hardships in their lives. We noticed that whenever they had an encounter with God during their grief, they found hope.

This devotional is divided into four sections. We've titled each section with a word from our acronym of HOPE: *Hear, Open, Prepare, Embrace.* These verbs are very important mile-markers for a journey from heartache to hope. If we are to move through our grief we must **hear** God's voice in our pain, **open** our hearts and minds to a change, **prepare** to do what God asks of us, and **embrace** God's presence in our trial.

You will notice we've added space for you to journal your own questions, answers, and prayers as you go along your way to help you apply the lessons you learn. There is no specific order or timeline that you need to follow in using this devotional. Please use it in whatever way helps you heal and find hope as you make your unique journey through your heartache.

As you read, we pray that you will find stories to help you understand where God is in your grief, and how he wants to help you move from heartache to hope.

Prologue

*O*ften, when a person in the Bible had an encounter with God, their lives were radically changed. You may find your life also radically changed when you let the encounters of hope in this devotional bring healing to your heartache.

However, you can also choose not to be changed when you encounter the divine. This is an example from the Bible about what can happen when we turn away from hope.

The Rich Young Ruler Turned Away from Hope

As Jesus was starting out on his way to Jerusalem, a man came running up to him, knelt down, and asked, "Good Teacher, what must I do to inherit eternal life?"

"Why do you call me good?" Jesus asked. "Only God is truly good. But to answer your question, you know the commandments: 'You must not murder. You must not commit adultery. You must not steal. You must not testify falsely. You must not cheat anyone. Honor your father and mother.'"

"Teacher," the man replied, "I've obeyed all these commandments since I was young."

Looking at the man, Jesus felt genuine love for him. "There is still one thing you haven't done," he told him. "Go and sell all your possessions and give the money to the poor, and you will have treasure in heaven. Then come, follow me."

At this the man's face fell, and he went away sad, for he had many possessions.

Mark 10:17-22 NLT

This is the story of a man who knew the law, and had kept it from his youth. He knew and did what God wanted from him. So when he approached Jesus and asked, "What must I do to inherit the Kingdom of heaven?" he was very surprised at the answer.

Heartache: Idolatry

Some people think this story is an example of why Christians shouldn't have wealth. I don't think this is the case. Perhaps this story is more about Jesus getting deep into the condition of this man's heart.

Jesus knew this man's heart just as he knows ours. He knew that this man loved his possessions more than he loved people. While Jesus doesn't ask everyone to give all of their riches to the poor, he does ask us to put the things of God above the things of the world. Allowing anything in your life to become more important to you than your relationship with God is the essence of idolatry.

Like the rich young ruler, we can know and do the right thing. On the surface we can look like good Christ-followers who go to church and read our Bibles. However, these actions are only outward indications of following Jesus. Jesus wants to go deeper with each of us as he did with the rich young ruler. He wants to address what is in our hearts.

Hope: The Kingdom of God

The rich young ruler chose to put his trust in his wealth and accomplishments instead of God. When Jesus asked him to put the Kingdom of God first, the man's face fell and he walked away from Jesus. He didn't want to put Jesus first. He wanted to hold on to his possessions, essentially making them idols in his life. And because he wasn't willing to let go of what he had, he turned his back on Jesus.

God may not be asking you to give up your wealth, but perhaps he has peered into your heart and found the thing that you keep as an idol. Maybe you hold on to being greedy or stingy. Perhaps you'd rather have prestige, reputation, or influence. Maybe you love your career or your family more than you love God. Anything that you value more than your relationship with Jesus can be an idol for you.

What are you holding deep in your heart? What do you keep locked away hoping that Jesus never demands it from you? Where are you putting desires for worldly things above what Jesus wants for you?

_____

_____

_____

_____

_____

_____

Don't turn away from your chance for hope! Spend some time in prayer asking God what he wants you to do for him.

Lord, I stand before you asking: What am I holding too tight? What do I need to let go of? What am I putting above you in my heart? Please open my eyes so I can let go of the idols in my life and put you first instead.

_____

_____

_____

_____

_____

_____

_____

_____

_____

_____

_____

_____

For more about the rich young ruler, read Mark 10:17-31 and Luke 18:18-30.

Hear

To make the journey between heartache and hope, we must first be willing to hear. Hearing the Word of God, a compassionate correction from a spiritual mentor, or a new way of thinking about what God wants will help us wrestle with our heartache.

We pray that you will listen and hear God speaking to you through the following stories.

- Hagar Heard God's Voice in Her Loneliness
- Jacob Heard Directly from God
- Deborah Heard God's Voice as She Faced the Enemy
- Samuel Heard a Disappointing Message from God
- Haggai Heard God's Correction
- Zechariah Heard a Special-Delivery Answer to Prayer
- Mary Sat at Jesus' Feet to Hear His Words
- Paul Heard God say "No"—Multiple Times!

Hagar Heard God's Voice in Her Loneliness

The LORD's messenger said to her, "Go back to your mistress. Put up with her harsh treatment of you." . . . "You are now pregnant and will give birth to a son. You will name him Ishmael [or God hears] because the LORD has heard about your harsh treatment."

Genesis 16:9, 11 CEB

We know very little about Hagar, but what we do know helps us expand our understanding of a very personal, deeply loving, and wonderfully inclusive God.

As a slave and a foreigner, Hagar had no rights, but that doesn't mean she didn't have dreams. Maybe she had hoped for a spouse among the other slaves. As a young woman, she may have dreamed of having children of her own. But when she was forced to become the surrogate for Sarah and Abraham, those dreams were dashed. Even the baby she was going to give birth to would be considered Sarah's child and not her own.

Heartache: Loss of the Dream of the "Perfect" Family

Hagar—an Egyptian slave girl—was the first person in Scripture to encounter the physical presence of the Angel of the Lord, whom many scholars believe was Jesus before he was in human form. That Angel was the only one in the story who called Hagar by her name. At the moment of Hagar's desperate loneliness, the Angel saw Hagar's plight and came to her. That Angel is the same God who sees our pain, too. The Angel who heard all the abusive words spewed out toward Hagar is the same God who hears the voices surrounding us. The Angel is the one who told Hagar what to name her son—Ishmael, which means "God hears." Hagar heard God speak to her. She took that news back to Abraham, who must've listened, because he indeed named his firstborn son, Ishmael.

And just as God provided abundantly for Hagar and her son in the middle of painfully difficult circumstances, the same God will provide for us and our imperfect families. And if we're listening for God's loving voice, we will begin to see the uniquely prepared, God-sized blessings awaiting us.

Hope: God will Bless the Family You *Have* (Not the One You Wished for)

While I can't imagine living in her circumstances with a verbally abusive mistress, I can imagine an encounter with a God who loves me. And while I know the pain of not having my own children or the "perfect family" for which I had once hoped, I have experienced the joy of "chosen" family.

What "family-type" joys have you experienced among your friends?

___

What hopes have you watched God fulfill in your family?

Lord, help me to hear your loving voice and be able to distinguish it from all the others that surround me.

For more of Hagar's story, read Genesis 16:1-15; 21:8-21; and 25:12-18

Jacob Heard Directly from God

> He had a dream in which he saw a stairway resting on the earth, with its top reaching to heaven, and the angels of God were ascending and descending on it. There above it stood the LORD, and he said: "I am the LORD, the God of your father Abraham and the God of Isaac. I will give you and your descendants the land on which you are lying. Your descendants will be like the dust of the earth, and you will spread out to the west and to the east, to the north and to the south. All peoples on earth will be blessed through you and your offspring. I am with you and will watch over you wherever you go, and I will bring you back to this land. I will not leave you until I have done what I have promised you."
>
> Genesis 28:11-15 NIV

Jacob was the son of Isaac, who betrayed his brother and stole the family birthright and blessing. He was also the father of the Jewish nation, who was seen by God and blessed by God. There is so much to the story of Jacob: Lessons to learn about how we should (or shouldn't) live, and how God works in our lives. This account helps us learn how an encounter with God can change our lives.

Heartache: Running Away

Jacob ran away in the night after he deceived his father, Isaac, into giving him a blessing that was meant for the firstborn, Esau. When Esau discovered Jacob's deceit, he threatened Jacob's life. So Jacob left in a hurry.

Do you remember when you were young, and you didn't like how things were going, so you packed your little backpack and decided that running away was the solution to everything? You may have even made it out the door and down the block before you realized that you couldn't cross the street. Or maybe you saw your mom or dad coming for you because they knew you needed them.

Maybe you want to run away from something as an adult—a hard relationship, a horrible job, or painful emotions. Perhaps, like Jacob, in running away you've run right to the place God will meet you.

Hope: An Encounter with God

God knows exactly what has happened and what we struggle with. These things aren't a surprise to him. Proverbs 16:9 says that although we might make our own plans, God knows our way and even directs our steps. So even when something bad happens and we try to run away from the repercussions, God knows. And he will meet us there.

In running away, Jacob came to the place where he could have a meaningful and life-changing encounter with God. He fell asleep and saw the heavens, hearing a message God had for him about blessing and abundance. God made a promise that through Jacob, God would fulfill his promise to Abraham. This changed Jacob to his core. Because of this encounter, Jacob no longer deceived others to get what he wanted.

If you read the rest of the story, you'll see that Jacob was later deceived and tricked by his uncle Laban. As a result, Jacob worked for Laban for many years in order to marry Rachel, the woman he loved. In this, we can see the evidence of Jacob's changed life. Jacob didn't try to deceive Laban. He was a good worker for 20 years and God blessed him abundantly, both financially and by making Jacob the father of the 12 tribes of Israel.

How could an encounter with God change you?

_____

_____

_____

_____

_____

_____

_____

_____

_____

_____

Lord, I feel like I am running and I don't know where I'm going. I'm running from who I used to be, and I want to be the person you desire. Will you show me who you are and what you have for me? I know an encounter with you could change my life!

For more on Jacob's life, read Genesis chapters 25-50.

Deborah Heard God's Voice as She Faced the Enemy

[Deborah] sent word to Barak,... "Hasn't the LORD, Israel's God, issued you a command?...'I'll lure Sisera, the commander of Jabin's army,...and then I'll help you overpower him.'"

Barak replied to her, "If you'll go with me, I'll go; but if not, I won't go."

Deborah answered, "I'll definitely go with you. However, the path you're taking won't bring honor to you, because the LORD will hand over Sisera to a woman." Then Deborah got up and went with Barak to Kedesh.

Judges 4:6-9 CEB

It is easy to understand how and why military battles cannot be fought alone. It takes an army of well-trained, willing fighters. And while most of us will not personally face a military battlefield, we will all face battles in life—whether it's a health challenge for ourselves or a loved one, a mental health crisis, a financial struggle, a disability, or any number of other difficulties that plague human existence. God has already provided others to help us along the way, but we may need to be humble enough to ask for that help.

Heartache: Facing a Battle She Couldn't Fight Alone

As a judge and national leader, Deborah was the well-respected, God-appointed, prophetic decision-maker over an unruly people. She even had to remind her military commander, Barak, of his responsibilities. She needed his help to win God's victory over their oppressor. Barak's reluctance to go into battle cost him his glory.

Instead of Barak winning the bravery medal, God allowed the woman Jael to kill their enemy's commander, while God sent the rains to muddy the land and thwart the power of the enemy army's chariots. Deborah's willingness to seek help and to collaborate with others to accomplish God's task brought 40 years of peace to her people.

Hope: Knowing God Would Provide Help from Others

Deborah's song of victory, one of the oldest poems in the Hebrew Bible, acknowledges God as the ultimate victor and also saves for posterity the names of others who fought on Israel's behalf. Deborah's faith in *God's* ability to overcome any challenge was only enhanced by the willing help of those around her.

What memories do you have of people who have helped you in the past?

_____

_____

_____

_____

_____

How have you acknowledged their partnership in getting you through tough times?

_____

_____

_____

_____

_____

Whom might God want you to ask to help you through a current challenge?

_____

_____

_____

_____

_____

Lord, open my eyes to the helpers you've placed in my path.

For more of Deborah's story, read Judges chapters 4-5.

Samuel Heard a Disappointing Message from God

When Samuel grew old, he appointed his sons as Israel's leaders. But his sons did not follow his ways. They turned aside after dishonest gain and accepted bribes and perverted justice.

So all the elders of Israel gathered together and came to Samuel at Ramah. They said to him, "You are old, and your sons do not follow your ways; now appoint a king to lead us, such as all the other nations have."

But when they said, "Give us a king to lead us," this displeased Samuel; so he prayed to the LORD. And the LORD told him: "Listen to all that the people are saying to you; it is not you they have rejected, but they have rejected me as their king. As they have done from the day I brought them up out of Egypt until this day, forsaking me and serving other gods, so they are doing to you. Now listen to them; but warn them solemnly and let them know what the king who will reign over them will claim as his rights.

1 Samuel 3:19-20 NRSV

Samuel got an early start learning to hear God's voice when he was just a child living at the tabernacle with the priest, Eli, who raised him. Samuel had been a faithful prophet of God his whole life. The Bible tells us that the Lord was with Samuel and he trusted Samuel.

So, you can imagine Samuel's surprise when not only were his sons rejected by the people as Israel's next leaders (and rightly so), but the people did not even want *God* to be their leader anymore. They wanted a king so they could be like the other nations around them.

Heartache: Rejection

I can sense the heartache Samuel must have experienced after a lifetime of faithfulness, trying to help the people hear and follow God's voice, only to be told by the people that they wanted a new system. And then probably even more confusing to Samuel at the time, God told him to listen to the people's request. *What?!* God was agreeing with this bunch of sinful people? However, as confusing as it may have seemed to him at the moment, Samuel knew how to follow God's instructions, and he did—to the letter.

Hope: Partnership with God

Once again, because Samuel knew how to discern God's voice, he was able to partner with God in a world-changing way. Surely Samuel's faithfulness had been nurtured as a child at the knee of his prayerful mother, Hannah. In that faithfulness, he was later able to discern just exactly who God wanted as king of Israel—not just the first time, but for the second king as well. Samuel's ability to hear God's voice changed the course of history—firstly, through King Saul and secondly, through

King David. Both of these men would be instrumental in providing the kind of leadership that God would use as instructive lessons for the ages. Because Samuel continued to listen to God's voice, even in the midst of his greatest heartaches, he influenced two kings, helped to shape a nation, and left a legacy of the power of faithful listening.

Sometimes, when we are at our most desperate moments, God is preparing us to partner with God in a world-changing way that we can't yet see or imagine.

What heartache has God brought you through in the past with a surprising outcome?

_____

_____

_____

_____

_____

_____

_____

_____

Have you considered how *your* faithfulness is influencing others in their ability to discern God's voice?

Lord, help me to listen for your voice and allow myself to be surprised by the hope only you can devise.

For more of Samuel's story, read the book of 1 Samuel.

Haggai Heard God's Correction

This is what the LORD Almighty says: "These people say, 'The time has not yet come to rebuild the LORD's house.'"

Then the word of the LORD came through the prophet Haggai: "Is it a time for you yourselves to be living in your paneled houses, while this house remains a ruin?"

Now this is what the LORD Almighty says: "Give careful thought to your ways. You have planted much, but harvested little. You eat, but never have enough. You drink, but never have your fill. You put on clothes, but are not warm. You earn wages, only to put them in a purse with holes in it."

Haggai 1:3-6 NIV

In the two chapters of the book of Haggai, the prophet tells how God reacted when the people of Israel, who were finally released from Babylon, ignored the work they were supposed to do in building the Temple. God told the people that they were still in so much distress because they were building up their own houses and ignoring God's Temple.

In my grief of dealing with infertility and miscarriages, God led me to the book of Haggai. His message to the Israelites to consider their ways helped me as I healed.

Heartache: Ignoring God

After a ruptured tubal pregnancy, losing our first-born son to a severe heart defect, and suffering five more miscarriages, I was angry with God. I couldn't understand why he would bring so much loss and grief into my life. So I closed my Bible and spent months trying to live on my own, in my own strength, trying to figure it out.

It may be a surprise to you, but this didn't work. I was angry all the time. I felt lost and empty. I did not like the person I was becoming. I missed the hope and peace that a life in God brings. So I opened my Bible again, turning to the book of Haggai.

As I read the Old Testament book of Haggai, New Testament verses about our bodies being the temple of the Holy Spirit came to mind. I realized I was neglecting God's spiritual temple within me the same way the Israelites were neglecting God's physical Temple, and my relationship with God was in ruins. I felt the Lord tell me, *"My temple in you is in ruins because you are ignoring your relationship with me."*

Just like the Israelites, I was neglecting God by putting my will before his, and it was drying me up. There was drought in my life because I refused to let God fill me.

Hope: Putting God First

Because of this reminder from Scripture, a light came on in my darkness. That light sparked a small flame that quickly ignited into a bonfire, burning up my doubt and anger, and chasing away my grief.

Just as God's Old Testament people realized they had neglected God and sought his forgiveness, I prayed for forgiveness and found peace. God was there, just waiting for me to realize how much I needed him.

God doesn't leave us when we are downtrodden. We usually leave him because we can't understand, in our limited perceptions, what he intends to accomplish through our trials. If you have been neglecting God, remember he has not abandoned you. He is simply waiting for you to call to him again.

How have you been neglecting your spiritual house?

_____

_____

_____

_____

_____

How might God be calling you to consider your ways?

_____

_____

_____

_____

_____

_____

Lord, I have considered my ways. Like the Israelites, I have lost my enthusiasm for you. I have put more energy and interest into what I want, not considering how I am neglecting my relationship with you. Forgive me and bring me back into your peace.

For more about this event, read Ezra chapters 1-5 and the book of Haggai in the Old Testament.

Zechariah Heard a Special-Delivery Answer to Prayer

In the time of Herod king of Judea there was a priest named Zechariah, who belonged to the priestly division of Abijah; his wife Elizabeth was also a descendant of Aaron. Both of them were righteous in the sight of God, observing all the Lord's commands and decrees blamelessly. But they were childless because Elizabeth was not able to conceive, and they were both very old…

Then an angel of the Lord appeared to him, standing at the right side of the altar of incense. When Zechariah saw him, he was startled and was gripped with fear. But the angel said to him: "Do not be afraid, Zechariah; your prayer has been heard. Your wife Elizabeth will bear you a son, and you are to call him John…

Zechariah asked the angel, "How can I be sure of this? I am an old man and my wife is well along in years."

The angel said to him, "I am Gabriel. I stand in the presence of God, and I have been sent to speak to you and to tell you this good news. And now you will be silent and not able to speak until the day this happens, because you did not believe my words, which will come true at their appointed time."

Luke 1:5-7, 11-13, 18-20 NIV

Heartache: First, Childlessness…Then, Muteness with Good News

The pain of childlessness had lasted throughout his marriage to Elizabeth. The whispered, judgmental comments from others had surely thickened his skin over the years. Regardless of the accusations and misunderstanding surrounding them, he and Elizabeth remained faithful to God and to each other through the years and through the pain.

Then, an angel appeared to share God's good news with Zechariah. As you can imagine, Zechariah was skeptical. Even if the answer to his prayer was being delivered by the angel Gabriel, the thought that his prayer for a son was actually being granted was a lot to swallow. After all, it was *physically* impossible—his wife, Elizabeth, was way past her childbearing years. Just to make sure Zechariah would eventually believe this, Gabriel caused Zechariah to go mute—unable to speak until the baby was born.

Zechariah was now carrying around the greatest news he'd ever heard and couldn't even speak it out loud. How frustrating! And in his day, that muteness was probably viewed as a punishment from God for some terrible sin. Instead, it was actually more evidence that the miracle was real.

Hope: Two Promises—Birth of a Son and Return of Voice for Prophetic Message

Can you picture the wildly animated scene when a mute Zechariah returned home to Elizabeth after his encounter with the angel Gabriel and his announcement of their soon-to-be parenthood? How fast can *you* write on a clay tablet? What were those next nine months like in that household? Quieter? More loving? More excited? Don't you wonder how busy they were with preparations for dreams coming true?

What have you had to endure while waiting for a prayer to be answered?

_____

_____

_____

_____

_____

How did these challenges make the answer just that much sweeter and more appreciated?

_____

_____

_____

_____

_____

Lord, give me the grace to work through my doubts and the trials that come while waiting for your glory to shine through.

For more about Zechariah's story, read Luke chapter 1.

Mary Sat at Jesus' Feet to Hear His Words

As Jesus and the disciples continued on their way to Jerusalem they came to a village where a woman named Martha welcomed them into her home. Her sister Mary sat on the floor, listening to Jesus as he talked. But Martha was the jittery type and was worrying over the big dinner she was preparing. She came to Jesus and said, "Sir, doesn't it seem unfair to you that my sister just sits here while I do all the work? Tell her to come and help me." But the Lord said to her, "Martha, dear friend, you are so upset over all these details! There is really only one thing worth being concerned about. Mary has discovered it—and I won't take it away from her!"

Luke 10:38-42 TLB

Looking at this story, I like to think Mary must have been the younger sister in this household, for she was more easily distracted from duty and gravitated toward other things, just like the youngest sibling sometimes does (that's just a guess on my part as the youngest sister in my family).

Heartache: Family Strife in the Face of Faith

We don't really know too much about any conversations Mary and Martha may have had in this interaction, but I'm sure Martha asked for Mary's help. Or maybe Mary knew what needed to be done, but was so enamored by Jesus that she couldn't leave his side. Let's use our imaginations and slip into Mary's day for a minute.

Mary may have been on her way to put fresh linens on the beds when she sees Jesus in the main room talking with his disciples. She has heard about this Jesus and the things he does. So she lingers in the doorway, holding the bed linens to her chest. Soon, she finds herself moving toward him. And then she lays down the linens on the floor by Jesus' feet and sits on them, listening to every word that comes from his mouth. She forgets all about helping Martha because she is hearing these amazing words of love and peace that come from Jesus.

I love what Jesus does here. Mary is sitting with Jesus, listening intently to his teaching. When Martha interrupts, Jesus does not condemn her for complaining; and neither does He condemn Mary for choosing to sit with him. What Jesus does is offer grace. He knows Martha's gifts and he knows Mary's heart. So even though Mary wasn't doing what Martha thought was best, Jesus gave grace and understanding to them both.

Hope: Jesus Gives Grace and Understanding

The Bible records another of Jesus' interactions with Mary and Martha in John 12:1-3. It says that Martha hosted a dinner in Jesus' honor, and while Martha served the food,

Mary sat at Jesus' feet, anointing him with perfume. This passage doesn't record any discord between the sisters. In the presence of Jesus, they each did what they were supposed to do, and neither sister bickered. This is the peace that comes with knowing Jesus.

There might be a time when you choose Jesus over a family relationship. Maybe your family doesn't understand your faith, or maybe they judge you for putting Jesus first. Take comfort in the hope that this interaction between Mary, Martha, and Jesus provides. Jesus will honor you for putting him first, and he will offer grace to your family member who may not understand.

Jesus said that spending time with Him is the most important thing. How will you let this give you hope when dealing with family members who don't understand your faith-based choices?

_____

_____

_____

_____

_____

_____

_____

_____

_____

Lord, choosing you is the most important thing. Help me remember this the next time I am with family members who don't understand and help me extend grace and peace to them as you did to Mary and Martha.

For more about Mary, the sister of Martha, read Luke chapter 10 and John chapter 11.

Paul Heard God Say "No" —Multiple Times!

Paul and his companions traveled throughout the region of Phrygia and Galatia, having been kept by the Holy Spirit from preaching the word in the province of Asia. When they came to the border of Mysia, they tried to enter Bithynia, but the Spirit of Jesus would not allow them to.
Acts 16:6-7 NIV

To keep me from thinking of myself as important, a thorn in the flesh was given to me, a messenger of Satan, to torment and harass me—to keep me from exalting myself! Concerning this I pleaded with the Lord three times that it might leave me; but He has said to me, "My grace is sufficient for you [My lovingkindness and My mercy are more than enough—always available—regardless of the situation]; for [My] power is being perfected [and is completed and shows itself most effectively] in [your] weakness." Therefore, I will all the more gladly boast in my weaknesses, so that the power of Christ [may completely enfold me and] may dwell in me. So I am well pleased with weaknesses, with insults, with distresses, with persecutions, and with difficulties, for the sake of Christ; for when I am weak [in human strength], then I am strong [truly able, truly powerful, truly drawing from God's strength].

2 Corinthians 12:7b-10 AMP

Heartache: Failed Plans and Painful Circumstances

Paul's dramatic conversion experience included going blind for a few days (see Acts chapter 9). Paul's work for God included redirected plans, shipwrecks, imprisonment, snake bites, beatings, and more. While those may seem a little extreme to us as modern-day Western Christians, we *can* all relate to well-thought-out plans falling apart, or tragic circumstances not being resolved, or hurtful things being said about us. We don't like it when we don't get our way, and we don't like being told "no." And yet, that's what God told Paul on numerous occasions.

Paul had experienced God's miraculous power to get him out of bad circumstances, so he could have expected God to deliver him from every negative situation. Yet, it was the painful circumstances that helped Paul to grow in his understanding of God's purposes.

Hope: God's Strength and Power Are Always Available

When Paul was redirected on his mission trips (as in Acts chapter 16), he took the gospel to places it hadn't gone before. When Paul suffered, others were able to see the power of God at work within him. Paul obviously learned that no matter the situation, there was a greater purpose than what he was able to see at the moment.

Every awful moment that causes pain and/or confusion is a moment when God's strength and power are accessible to you. Paul's testimony can become your testimony.

When is a time you were frustrated with God and then later realized how God had prevented an even greater heartache?

_____

_____

_____

_____

_____

_____

When is a time you felt God was unfair, yet you learned a valuable lesson in the process?

_____

_____

_____

_____

_____

_____

Lord, help me to depend on the sufficiency—the more-than-enoughness—of your grace and strength whenever life gets hard.

For more of this particular incident in Paul's life, read 2 Corinthians chapter 12.

OPEN

When on a journey from heartache to hope, we must be open to the lessons God has for us. Being open to new ways of thinking, to doing the right thing, or even being open to the experiences God wants us to have will help us grow.

We pray that you will be open to whatever lessons God wants you to learn through these devotionals.

- Esau was Open to Forgiving after a Deep Betrayal
- Joshua was Open to God's Power to Prevail
- Naomi was Open to Help
- Nehemiah Opened Himself to Ridicule to Show God's Power
- Elizabeth Opened Her Life to Someone Else's Joy
- Jairus was Open to Having Faith
- A Woman Caught in Adultery was Open to Jesus' Compassion
- The Man Born Blind was Open to God's Purpose
- Mary Magdalene Opened Herslef to a New Reality
- Lydia Opened Her Home at the Risk of Her Livelihood

Esau Was Open to Forgiving after a Deep Betrayal

> Jacob looked up and there was Esau, coming with his four hundred men; so he divided the children among Leah, Rachel and the two female servants. He put the female servants and their children in front, Leah and her children next, and Rachel and Joseph in the rear. He himself went on ahead and bowed down to the ground seven times as he approached his brother. But Esau ran to meet Jacob and embraced him; he threw his arms around his neck and kissed him. And they wept.
>
> Genesis 33:1-4 NIV

If you have been in church very long, you will likely have heard the story of Esau and Jacob; twins born to Isaac and Rebecca, whom God said would live in strife. Esau, the eldest of the twins (and therefore the rightful heir) sold his birthright to Jacob for a bowl of stew. Jacob then stole Esau's blessing from their dying father. So through betrayal and conniving, Jacob, who was second-born, received both the inheritance and the first-born blessing from his father.

Heartache: Deep Betrayal

Of the many things this account teaches us, an important lesson is that rivalry and betrayal can ruin a family.

Maybe you have been betrayed by a family member. Perhaps they lied, or took something that belonged to you. Maybe they disrespected you or ruined your relationship somehow. There are many ways family members can hurt one another. Betrayal by a family member is most hurtful because we expect the people in our family to know us best and easily forgive us for our shortcomings. However, this isn't always what happens.

In the Scripture account of the beginning of this story, Esau had his birthright and blessing stolen by Jacob, so Esau chased his brother out of town. Many years later, Esau heard that his brother was on his way back with many people, possessions, and livestock. Not knowing if Jacob was coming to start a war, Esau headed out with 400 of his men to meet him.

Hope: Forgiving Restores Relationships

As Esau was traveling toward his brother, he encountered groups of men, each with a gift for him from Jacob. After many of these encounters, Esau finally saw Jacob and his tribe. He rode quickly towards his brother and dismounted his horse. Then, Esau ran to Jacob, who was bowing in the sand, and hugged him, bringing both of them to tears.

The Bible never says why Esau forgave his brother. Maybe he was more mature, or maybe God worked in Esau's life and he saw that things worked themselves out for the best. But that is only conjecture. What I do know is that the brother who didn't deserve forgiveness was completely and freely forgiven by Esau, who had every right to hold a grudge forever. This is a beautiful example that forgiveness can restore relationships, regardless of how egregious the offense is.*

Forgiveness can bring a family back together. It restores relationships and heals deep wounds.

Who in your life needs the hope of forgiveness?

_____

_____

_____

_____

_____

_____

How can you show that you have forgiven the offense and welcome that person back into your life?

_____

_____

_____

_____

_____

_____

Lord, forgiveness is hard. Sometimes betrayals are deep. But I understand how much you have forgiven me, so I ask that you help me forgive _____ for their betrayal.

_____

_____

_____

_____

_____

_____

_____

_____

_____

_____

_____

_____

For more on this account of Esau and his brother, read Genesis chapters 27, 32, and 33.

*Note: There are some acts of betrayal that are harder to forgive on your own. There is no denying that sometimes forgiveness takes a long time and may even require family or individual counseling. If this is the case for you, consider getting professional help from a counselor or pastor who can help you work through forgiveness. It may not be easy, but it is always better to forgive the one who betrayed you.

Joshua Was Open to God's Power to Prevail

> Joshua son of Nun and Caleb son of Jephunneh, who were among those who had explored the land, tore their clothes and said to the entire Israelite assembly, "The land we passed through and explored is exceedingly good. If the LORD is pleased with us, he will lead us into that land, a land flowing with milk and honey, and will give it to us. Only do not rebel against the LORD. And do not be afraid of the people of the land, because we will devour them. Their protection is gone, but the LORD is with us. Do not be afraid of them."
>
> But the whole assembly talked about stoning them.
>
> Numbers 14:6-10a NIV

Joshua was one of 12 scouts sent out by Moses to survey the territory God had promised would be their homeland. Upon their return they gave a report of the bountifulness of the land—and of its strong inhabitants who outnumbered them. Ten of the 12 scouts were then too fearful to pursue the land and their rumors among the people caused them all to doubt God's power. Only Joshua and Caleb had the faith that God's plan would ultimately prevail.

Heartache: Disbelieved by Majority of Peers

Those who doubted God's power were denied the opportunity to ever live in the land God had promised them, and they had to live the next 40 years wandering in the wilderness. Only Joshua's and Caleb's families would survive long enough to enter the Promised Land.

Joshua's courage came from his trust in God's power and his dependence on God's Law. He knew that he was just an instrument and that God was the true victor.

Hope: Strength and Courage from God's Word/Law

Joshua got a personal word from God to encourage him. We may desire such a thing…but, wait! We already have it. Joshua did not have a Bible. We do. We have constant access to all of God's promises in the palms of our hands. We can claim the promises to Joshua as our own. Here is what God said to Joshua:

> No one will be able to stand against you all the days of your life. As I was with Moses, so I will be with you; I will never leave you nor forsake you. Be strong and courageous, because you will lead these people to inherit the land I swore to their ancestors to give them.
>
> Be strong and very courageous. Be careful to obey all the law my servant Moses gave you; do not turn from it to the right or to the left, that you may be successful wherever you go.
>
> Joshua 1:5-7 NIV

The truth we glean from God's Word will help us stand strong in our faith—even when others' doubts could bring us down. God's Word brings encouragement when we're hurting, hope when we're disappointed, and strength when we think we just can't go on.

Have you ever felt like the lone voice of truth, or faced unbelief from your peers?

_____

_____

_____

_____

_____

_____

From where can you draw the strength to stand your ground?

_____

_____

_____

_____

_____

_____

_____

Lord, fill my heart and mind with the truth of your Word so that I may be able to discern your voice above all others and can overcome the doubt with which others try to block my way.

___

For more of Joshua's story, read the book of Joshua.

Naomi Was Open to Help

> With her two daughters-in-law she left the place where she had been living and set out on the road that would take them back to the land of Judah. Then Naomi said to her two daughters-in-law, "Go back, each of you, to your mother's home. May the LORD show you kindness, as you have shown kindness to your dead husbands and to me. May the LORD grant that each of you will find rest in the home of another husband." Then she kissed them goodbye and they wept aloud.
> Ruth 1:7-9 NIV

The story of Ruth and Naomi is well-known from Ruth's point of view, but Naomi faced much heartbreak on her journey to hope, and it is sometimes left unexplored. Naomi's husband died, as did her two sons, leaving her and her two daughters-in-law without any resources in Moab, where they lived. Naomi decided it was best to go back to the land of her people in Bethlehem and she urged Ruth and Orpah to go back to their own families. Ruth refused and ended up helping herself and Naomi survive.

Heartache: Being Alone

Although Naomi's story is about being a widow, there is also wider application to those who are alone in life for any reason. Naomi's husband and sons died, leaving her to fend for herself in a world where a woman could not get honorable work and have often had to depend on others for help.

You may have lost a spouse, but that is not the only reason you may find yourself alone. You could be new to a community. You could be estranged or separated from family members. You could be experiencing loneliness or depression. Whatever has brought you to a state of being alone, the fact remains that you *feel* alone. Maybe even lost. And that is a heartache that is hard to bear.

Naomi felt so lost and alone that she changed her name from Naomi, meaning "sweet" or "pleasant," to Mara, meaning "bitter." She was angry that this had happened to her, and she was especially angry at God for allowing it.

Hope: God Does Not Abandon Us

Even though Naomi was angry with God, he was still working in her life. He did not abandon her. He had a great plan for redemption in this story, and not only for Naomi, but for everyone. (See the entry on Ruth.)

Because Naomi trusted in the laws of the Torah, which came from God, she was taken care of by a kinsman through the help of Ruth. Our faith in God gives us strength and resilience.

Naomi's faith was also bolstered by other believers. Ruth clung to Naomi, claiming Naomi as her family and Naomi's people as her own. Because she had Ruth helping her, Naomi didn't starve, and she eventually had a home.

Naomi's story helps us see that when we remain faithful to God, he will provide restoration and redemption. It may not be immediately, but no matter how long it takes, trusting God is never in vain. He will always restore us, help us, and take care of us.

Has your faith been tested recently? How will you remain faithful to God and allow him to care for you and bring you into his grace?

_____

_____

_____

_____

_____

_____

_____

_____

_____

_____

_____

Lord, thank you for showing me that I am not alone in feeling alone. I can see that you are here with me, and that my faith in you will get me through any heartache I have. Thank you for saving me and taking care of me in all my circumstances.

For more on this story, read the book of Ruth in the Old Testament.

Nehemiah Opened Himself to Ridicule to Show God's Power

When Sanballat heard that we were rebuilding the wall, he became angry and was greatly incensed. He ridiculed the Jews…

Hear us, our God, for we are despised. Turn their insults back on their own heads. Give them over as plunder in a land of captivity. Do not cover up their guilt or blot out their sins from your sight, for they have thrown insults in the face of the builders.

So we rebuilt the wall till all of it reached half its height, for the people worked with all their heart.

Nehemiah 4:1, 4-6 NIV

When all our enemies heard about this, all the surrounding nations were afraid and lost their self-confidence, because they realized that this work had been done with the help of our God.

Nehemiah 6:16 NIV

Nehemiah was a leader who knew how to organize the people to accomplish an overwhelming task—to rebuild the walls of Jerusalem in the presence of opposing nations with bigger armies. All the while, Nehemiah and the people faced constant ridicule and hardships. Many leaders would simply give up because it was almost impossible to maintain the spirits of the workers to get the job done. In spite of the opposition, Nehemiah faced down the bullies—but not alone.

Heartache: Opposition to His Leadership

Nehemiah held fast to the fact that the king he worked for had authorized his work and had even provided the supplies. He believed in the abilities of the Israelites to do the work. He trusted in the power of God to overcome any obstacle thrown their way, and he stayed focused on his responsibility to keep the people organized and motivated, even in the face of opposition.

Hope: Confidence in God's Call and Power

Much to the amazement of all the naysayers, the wall around the city was rebuilt in just 52 days! The rebuilding of their Temple and their wall brought the people cause for much celebration of the power of God to strengthen and sustain them regardless of the fierceness of any enemy's attack.

Leadership requires opening yourself to face opposition—and maybe even ridicule—at some point. How you handle opposition will reveal your true self. Are you *too weak* to withstand it on your own, or are you *weak enough* to acknowledge your dependence on God's Spirit within you to fulfill the calling on your life?

What obstacles to personal accomplishments have you faced in the past?

How did you rely on God and/or the support of others around you to push through those obstacles?

If this is a challenging thing for you to do, who are some Christian leaders you know from whom you could learn?

Lord, give me the wisdom to identify the true source of obstacles in my way and your strength to overcome them.

For more of Nehemiah's story, read the books of Ezra and Nehemiah.

Elizabeth Opened Her Life to Someone Else's Joy

[Elizabeth said,] "This is the Lord's doing. He has shown his favor to me by removing my disgrace among other people"…

[The angel Gabriel said to Mary,] "Look, even in her old age, your relative Elizabeth has conceived a son. This woman who was labeled 'unable to conceive' is now six months pregnant. Nothing is impossible for God"…Mary got up and hurried to a city in the Judean highlands…

With a loud voice [Elizabeth] blurted out [to Mary], "God has blessed you above all women, and he has blessed the child you carry. Why do I have this honor, that the mother of my Lord should come to me? As soon as I heard your greeting, the baby in my womb jumped for joy. Happy is she who believed that the Lord would fulfill the promises he made to her."
Luke 1:25, 36-37, 39, 42-45 CEB

Heartache: Disapproval from Others

Elizabeth had been scorned and shamed her whole married life because she was unable to have children. Unfortunately, the ruling thought of the day was that barrenness, or infertility, was God's punishment. Since Elizabeth's husband, Zechariah, was a priest, we can only imagine the rumors that circulated about their childlessness. Yet, the gospel writer Luke made it clear that they were both righteous before God (see Luke 1:6).

Then God did a miracle (or two or three) and she and Zechariah were finally expecting their first child—in their old age! What joy! What vindication! What rearranging of their lives! And just about the time they were to start on the nursery, her much younger, unwed, pregnant niece Mary showed up! To make matters even worse, Mary was at risk of being stoned to death for this pregnancy. In the midst of Elizabeth's ultimate joy and excitement, she was now put at risk for housing a pregnant, unwed teenager. Talk about disapproval!

Thankfully, Elizabeth was in tune with the Holy Spirit and got immediate reassurance that Mary's pregnancy was also a God-breathed miracle. Elizabeth's spirit was prompted to voice the first word of prophecy after 400 years of God's prophetic silence and she confirmed that Mary was carrying the long-awaited Messiah.

Hope: God's Plan Always Includes a Unique Role for Each of Us

Elizabeth now understood that the purpose of those painful years was to prepare her for this moment of multiplied joy—her own pregnancy as well as the honor of hosting the mother-to-be of the promised Savior. Elizabeth could have been jealous—why would

God choose this unwed teenager over her to birth the Messiah? Instead, we get to witness Elizabeth's ecstatic wonder. We are allowed to ponder the intimate moments during their three-month visit. My heart tells me that Elizabeth gently prepared Mary for the scorn and shame she would surely face as others would question her pregnancy and the legitimacy of her son. Elizabeth opened her life to Mary's joy and basked in the unique roles God had for each of them.

How can you make room in your very full life to be ready to enter into someone else's joy or pain?

_____

_____

_____

_____

_____

Who could benefit from your wisdom and experience as you celebrate God's activity in her life?

_____

_____

_____

_____

_____

Lord, help me make room in my life—regardless of my circumstances—for others' joy or pain.

For more of Elizabeth's story, read Luke chapter 1.

Jairus Was Open to Having Faith

> Then one of the synagogue leaders, named Jairus, came, and when he saw Jesus, he fell at his feet. He pleaded earnestly with him, "My little daughter is dying. Please come and put your hands on her so that she will be healed and live." So Jesus went with him…

[As he was going, Jesus had an encounter with the woman with a bleeding disorder.]

> While Jesus was still speaking, some people came from the house of Jairus, the synagogue leader. "Your daughter is dead," they said. "Why bother the teacher anymore?"
> Overhearing what they said, Jesus told him, "Don't be afraid; only have faith."
> Mark 5:22-24, 35-36 NIV

Jairus was a leader in the synagogue who had undoubtedly heard that Jesus was able to heal the sick. So he ignored the opinions of the other leaders and went to find Jesus. He approached Jesus with the request that Jesus heal his daughter. And Jesus went with him. I believe Jairus was overjoyed that Jesus was going to help him.

Heartache: Disappointment in God's Timing

On the way to Jairus' house, Jesus stopped and had an encounter with a woman who had been sick for years. As Jesus is helping that woman, someone came from Jairus' household saying his daughter had died. Jairus' heart must have broken. It was too late. His daughter would not be healed.

Having had one of my own children die, I can feel the despair that was in Jairus' heart. Maybe he thought, *"If only I'd come sooner,"* or, *"If only Jesus hadn't lingered."* The hope for his daughter's healing was lost.

Hope: Faith

In verse 36, Mark writes that Jesus overheard the messenger's news for Jairus so Jesus turned to Jairus and said, "Don't be afraid; only have faith."

Only have faith.

When the world falls apart. When death is at the door. When nothing makes sense. When the timing seems hopeless. Jesus says, "Only have faith."

He makes it seem easy. *Just have faith that everything will be okay.*

What does that kind of faith look like?

Having faith means following Jesus anyway. In this story, Jairus followed Jesus back to his house even though the messenger said it was too late (verse 37). In our own story, maybe having faith means continuing to do the things Jesus asks us to do: read the Bible, go to church, pray, and worship God even when our hopes are dashed.

Having faith means dealing with laughter and ridicule. In verses 39-40 of this story, Jesus came to Jairus' house and said, "Why all this commotion and weeping? The child isn't dead; she's only asleep." When they heard those words, the crowd laughed. In our own story, we may have to endure the mockery of others who don't understand our faith. They may make fun of us or call us weak-minded. Having faith may mean enduring scorn.

Having faith means looking at the problem with confidence and trusting that Jesus has the answer. Jairus trusted Jesus, regardless of what his peers said. He believed Jesus would help him and that faith gave him hope. In our own story, we may not understand why things happen the way they do, but we can trust that Jesus will help us.

Jesus wants us to be open to having the faith that he will do what needs to be done and his timing will be right. He wants us to let go of fear and trust him.

Where in your life is Jesus telling you, "Do not be afraid; only have faith"?

_____

_____

_____

_____

_____

_____

_____

_____

Lord, you know my every need. Help me not be afraid, and instead be open to embracing faith and believe that you will do what is best in this situation.

For the whole story of Jairus and his daughter, read Mark 5:22-43.

A Woman Caught in Adultery Was Open to Jesus' Compassion

As he was speaking, the teachers of religious law and the Pharisees brought a woman who had been caught in the act of adultery. They put her in front of the crowd. "Teacher," they said to Jesus, "this woman was caught in the act of adultery. The law of Moses says to stone her. What do you say?" They were trying to trap him into saying something they could use against him, but Jesus stooped down and wrote in the dust with his finger.

They kept demanding an answer, so he stood up again and said, "All right, but let the one who has never sinned throw the first stone!" Then he stooped down again and wrote in the dust. When the accusers heard this, they slipped away one by one, beginning with the oldest, until only Jesus was left in the middle of the crowd with the woman. Then Jesus stood up again and said to the woman, "Where are your accusers? Didn't even one of them condemn you?"

"No, Lord," she said.

And Jesus said, "Neither do I. Go and sin no more."

John 8:3–11 NLT

The condemnation of a crowd can feel threatening. Imagine being this woman, pulled out into the Temple courtyard to have your sin displayed in front of everyone. As the frenzy of the crowd grows, everyone begins picking up rocks to throw at you. No one is listening to your story. They just want to judge you and condemn you.

In the United States, we are not stoned to death for our sins. But the fear of being found out can cause us to hide our sins. We pretend everything is okay on the outside when our lives are really rotting away because of unconfessed sin and the burden of keeping it hidden. This fear and anxiety can cause us to turn away from God or the community of our church because we don't want to be condemned for our sins.

Heartache: Sin and Shame

We all sin. The Bible says no one on their own is righteous (see Romans 3:10). Thankfully, God gives us an avenue to confess our sins and be forgiven. 1 John 1:9 says, "If we confess our sins, he is faithful and just and will forgive us our sins and purify us from all unrighteousness." (NIV)

Still, we carry around shame for sins that *feel* bigger. These are sins we don't want others to know about. And the thing about hiding sins is that they will eventually be found out. We will be caught, someone will call us out, or the Holy Spirit will convict us.

No one will be innocent of sin when we stand in front of God. But the presence of Jesus changes things. He brings compassion, forgiveness, and the power to stop sinning.

Hope: Compassion and Forgiveness

When the religious leaders brought the adulterous woman to Jesus, he answered the demands of the crowd out of compassion for the sinner. He offered to let anyone without sin to cast the first stone. In truth, Jesus was the *only* one without sin, yet he did not pick up a stone. Instead, he waited. Soon, the crowd walked away, as they were each confronted by their own sins. After a while, Jesus looked up at the woman and told her that she was forgiven and free to go and sin no more.

Jesus came to this world to save us, not condemn us. No matter what sin you may be holding on to, hiding in, or burying because of shame, Jesus will give you mercy and forgiveness. He will not throw stones when you come to him. Instead, he will offer you new life.

The presence of Jesus changes everything. He washes away the old and makes us new. He can give us a life filled with peace if we will only come to him with our shame and be open to his compassion.

Are there secret sins in your life that feel heavy and shameful? Come to Jesus and ask for forgiveness. He will trade your shame for peace.

Lord, forgive me of my sins. Wash away all that I have done wrong and cover me in your compassion and mercy. Help me live a new life in you.

___

___

___

___

___

___

___

___

___

___

___

___

___

___

For the complete story of the adulterous woman, read John 7:53-8:11.

The Man Born Blind Was Open to God's Purpose

As Jesus was walking along, he saw a man who had been blind from birth. "Rabbi," his disciples asked him, "why was this man born blind? Was it because of his own sins or his parents' sins?"

"It was not because of his sins or his parents' sins," Jesus answered. "This happened so the power of God could be seen in him."

John 9:1-3 NLT

During Jesus' time on this earth people believed that illness or disabilities happened because of personal sin. Certainly sin can lead to suffering, but suffering is not always caused by sin. Sometimes painful things happen that are out of our control but God can, and will, use them for His glory.

Heartache: Living with a Health Issue

We don't know much about this man and his family except that he was a beggar on the side of the road. He didn't have any other opportunity to earn a living as a blind person.

Here's what I find most encouraging about this story: Jesus saw the man and knew his circumstances. He didn't have to ask the man how long he had been blind or how it happened. Jesus knew he was blind from birth. And he knew that God's power would be seen in this man's circumstance.

After the man was healed, the religious leaders went after both him and his family. They demanded to know if Jesus was from God or if he was a heretic. Finally, after hours of questioning, the man said to the leaders, "Ever since the world began, no one has been able to open the eyes of someone born blind. If this man were not from God, he couldn't have done it" (John 9:32-33 NLT).

And there was the purpose for his blindness—he glorified God.*

Hope: God Will Use Your Circumstances for His Glory

We live in a world that is full of challenging circumstances, health issues being just one example. There are some things you can be certain about in your circumstances. First, outside of consequences from abusing your body, God does not inflict health problems on you because of sin. Your illness is not a judgment on your behavior. It is not condemnation from God. Second, there is comfort for anyone who is suffering. Jesus sees you and cares for you. He knows the why and the how, and he wants to become involved in this part of your story. And third, God never does anything directly to harm you, but he can use challenging circumstances to help you grow. As you grow, you can glorify him for providing the strength to carry on, for the lessons he's taught about his grace and love, and for the peace he gives you in your pain.

Having a lingering or chronic health issue is hard. Maybe you were born with a disability or illness or maybe it developed later in life and you haven't been able to find relief. But take heart; God can use your circumstances to reveal His power. The question is, will you let him?

What are some specific ways you have seen evidence of God's presence or power in the midst of God's suffering?

_____

_____

_____

_____

_____

_____

_____

_____

_____

_____

_____

_____

Lord, I surrender my circumstances to you and ask that your power be revealed to those around me.

_____

_____

_____

_____

_____

_____

_____

_____

_____

Read more about the man who was born blind in John chapter 9.

A special note to those still waiting for healing:

Healing can look different than we expect. Sometimes it looks like acceptance. Sometimes it looks like not letting fear have a grip on our lives. And sometimes healing is simply embracing that we are loved and called children of God. When we glorify God for giving us the strength to carry on, that still fulfills the words of Jesus: "This happened so the power of God could be seen in him (or her)." (John 9:3 NLT)

Mary Magdalene Opened Herself to a New Reality

[Mary]…saw Jesus standing there but she did not realize that it was Jesus. He asked, "Woman, why are you crying? Who is it you are looking for?"

Thinking he was the gardener, she said, "Sir, if you have carried him away, tell me where you have put him, and I will get him."

Jesus said to her, "Mary."

She turned toward him and cried out in Aramaic, "Rabboni!" (Which means "Teacher")…

Jesus said, "Do not hold on to me, for I have not yet ascended to the Father. Go instead to my brothers and tell them, 'I am ascending to my Father and your Father, to my God and your God.'"

Mary Magdalene went to the disciples with the news: "I have seen the Lord!" And she told them that he had said these things to her.

John 20:14-17 NIV

When it comes to loyalty, you cannot find another person in Scripture who was more steadfast in his or her commitment to Jesus than Mary Magdalene. From the moment Jesus healed her of seven demons, she immediately began financially supporting and traveling with Jesus and his male disciples (see Luke 8:1-3). *That* had to raise some eyebrows! Nevertheless, Jesus obviously welcomed it.

Heartache: Death of a Dream—The Loss of a Loved One and All You Would Share

That loyalty had a painful price. She had placed all her hope in Jesus and the life he offered her, only to watch him be falsely accused and executed by crucifixion. She stood by him till the end—at the cross and even to the tomb. Only after he was buried and it was time for the Sabbath rituals did she leave his side. Her first love was gone. What would she do now? The reality of a new life of peace and service to others seemed impossible.

Hope: Birth of an Even Better Dream

Of all the people Jesus could have—and some would argue, should have—appeared to after his resurrection, he consciously chose to appear *first* to Mary Magdalene. Then, he commissioned her to be the first person to announce the greatest news in history: Christ is risen!! The social code of the day would prevent any male hearers from believing a woman's testimony, and yet, Jesus had full confidence in her.

Can you imagine the shock of seeing someone risen from the dead, let alone talking to him and getting an assignment from him? Think for a moment of all the ideas and plans that may have raced through her mind: *What will this mean for my future? For the ministry's future? This is a good thing—isn't it? Wait, what if no one believes me? Will Jesus finally overthrow the Romans? What will his mother say when I tell her?*

We don't know all the thoughts Mary had, but we do know she went and told the disciples as the first witness to the resurrection and then they had to grapple with this new reality. Her hopes were now limitless—she had just experienced the risen Christ!

What might God want to do through *you*—even after the painful loss of a loved one?

_____

_____

_____

_____

_____

_____

_____

_____

_____

_____

_____

Lord, help me to see with new eyes all the possibilities that you have for my life.

For more of Mary Magdalene's story, read Matthew chapters 27-28; Mark chapters 15-16; Luke chapters 8 and 24; and John chapters 19-20.

Lydia Opened Her Home at the Risk of Her Livelihood

One of those women was Lydia, a Gentile God-worshipper from the city of Thyatira, a dealer in purple cloth. As she listened, the Lord enabled her to embrace Paul's message. Once she and her household were baptized, she urged, "Now that you have decided that I am a believer in the Lord, come and stay in my house." And she persuaded us…

When Paul and Silas had been severely beaten, the authorities threw them into prison and ordered the jailer to secure them with great care…Around midnight Paul and Silas were praying and singing hymns to God, and the other prisoners were listening to them. All at once there was such a violent earthquake that it shook the prison's foundations. The doors flew open and everyone's chains came loose…

Paul and Silas left the prison and made their way to Lydia's house where they encouraged the brothers and sisters. Then they left Philippi.

Acts 16:14-15, 23, 25-26, 40 CEB

As a God-fearer, Lydia had already made the transition from her Gentile lifestyle to the point of believing in the God of the Jews. God was at work in her heart, preparing her to hear the gospel presented by Paul.

Based on the description of Lydia as a dealer in purple cloth, the mention of her whole household being baptized, and her invitation to Paul and Silas to come and stay at her house, we can deduce that she was a financially successful businesswoman. Purple cloth was worn mainly by royalty and the extremely wealthy, so the majority of her clientele was probably influential Romans, not Jews.

Heartache: Potential Loss of Livelihood

So, we can imagine that when Paul and Silas—these religious newcomers who came to town—were arrested and thrown in prison, the fact that Lydia was associated with them could have negatively impacted her reputation and her business. There is no mention of a husband, so it is likely that she is solely responsible for her household and employees. Her relationship with these "criminals" could result in the loss of her livelihood and of her employees' livelihoods.

While the Scriptures don't let us hear her voice any of those concerns, it is logical to assume that she had them. The fear of the loss of your job is real and can disrupt your life, your relationships, and your work performance.

Hope: Fellowship with God's Church

This is where the benefits of having a church family really come to light! The church family that was growing in Lydia's home would have been a wonderful encouragement to her and apparently a place of refuge for the recently released Paul and Silas.

How has your church family blessed you? Are you making it a habit to invite others to share in the blessings of your church family?

_____

_____

_____

_____

_____

_____

_____

_____

_____

_____

_____

_____

Lord, help me to function in the assurance that my church family loves me and can be my first source of encouragement whenever life's trials come my way.

For more of Lydia's story, read Acts chapter 16, and then read Paul's letter to the Philippians to get a sense of the close relationship Paul had with the church that started in Lydia's home.

Prepare

Another step in the journey from heartache to hope involves being prepared: being prepared for a new direction, a new attitude, or a new encounter. If we prepare our hearts for whatever God has in store for us on our journey, we will be more receptive to what he is doing in our lives.

We pray that you will prepare your heart and your mind for whatever message God gives you in the following pages.

- Miriam Prepared to Lead Others in Worship
- Joseph Was Prepared for Leadership Through Trials
- Ruth Prepared to Help
- David Prepared His Heart
- Huldah Prepared to Speak the Difficult Truth from God's Word
- Anna Prepared to See the Long-Awaited Savior by Worshiping Daily
- The Samaritan Woman Was Prepared to Discuss Deeply Troubling Questions
- The Sick Woman Prepared for Healing

Miriam Prepared to Lead Others in Worship

Then the prophet Miriam, Aaron's sister, took a tambourine in her hand. All the women followed her playing tambourines and dancing. Miriam sang the refrain back to them: Sing to the LORD, for an overflowing victory! Horse and rider he threw into the sea!

Exodus 15:20-21 CEB

The Bible doesn't reveal to us any of Miriam's earlier songs of praise, but I can imagine that she learned early in life how to praise God for his protection. After all, she had been there as a young girl when her baby brother Moses was rescued from the Nile river by Pharaoh's daughter. She had even been brave enough to approach Pharaoh's daughter and suggest a Hebrew nurse for the infant, which resulted in Moses being raised by his own mother and later adopted into Egypt's most powerful family. What a miracle! Miriam had witnessed God's hand at work in her family and it had prepared her heart for praise.

Heartache: A Difficult Journey Ahead with No Immediate Answers

Decades later, she helped that baby brother of hers and her other younger brother Aaron to lead the Hebrews out of slavery and out of Egypt. And just at the moment when they thought they were finally free, Pharaoh's army came barreling down on them. Can you imagine the thoughts that ran through her mind?

Have we survived all those plagues just to be trapped in this desert with nowhere to run?

And even if we do win this battle, how much longer can we survive out here in the desert?

Does Moses have all this figured out yet?

Will God really fulfill the promise of a new homeland?

Then, just as she had watched God save Moses from a watery grave when he was an infant, she witnessed God's power again. This time, God pushed back the waters of the Red Sea to save all of her people.

Hope: Witnessed God's Miracle at the Brink of Death

Miriam had much to sing about. Her joy overflowed to others to the point of her song being preserved through the centuries! Miriam's story provides us with the identity of the Bible's first praise and worship leader—a woman with a tambourine. What had seemed hopeless was now a testimony for the ages!

What evidence do you have that God has provided for you in the past?

_____

_____

_____

_____

_____

_____

_____

How can your praise of the all-powerful God's acts of the past give your heart hope for what God is capable of now?

_____

_____

_____

_____

_____

_____

_____

_____

Lord, help me sing your praise even when I can't see the end of my journey.

For more of Miriam's story—the only woman in Scripture about whom we can read of her childhood and her death —read Exodus chapter 2, 15, Numbers chapters 12, 20, 26; Deuteronomy 24:9; 1 Chronicles 6:3; and Micah 6:4.

Joseph Was Prepared for Leadership Through Trials

But while Joseph was there in the prison, the LORD was with him; he showed him kindness and granted him favor in the eyes of the prison warden.

When two full years had passed, Pharaoh had a dream: ...So Pharaoh sent for Joseph...Pharaoh said to Joseph, "I had a dream, and no one can interpret it. But I have heard it said of you that when you hear a dream you can interpret it."

"I cannot do it," Joseph replied to Pharaoh, "but God will give Pharaoh the answer he desires"...Then Joseph said to Pharaoh, "The dreams of Pharaoh are one and the same. God has revealed to Pharaoh what he is about to do...

Then Pharaoh said to Joseph, "Since God has made all this known to you, there is no one so discerning and wise as you. You shall be in charge of my palace, and all my people are to submit to your orders. Only with respect to the throne will I be greater than you."

Genesis 39:20-21; 41:1-40 NIV

Joseph's story has been made into movies and musicals. He is the poster boy for riches to rags to riches. Yes, God eased Joseph's trials, but that is not to say his journey was easy. As a young boy, his older brothers sold him into slavery because they were tired of his arrogance. Then, they lied to their father and told him that Joseph had been killed by a wild animal. What scoundrels! However, if you read the whole story, you'll discover there was a brief time of poetic justice and then there was an abundance of forgiveness and reconciliation.

Heartache: False Accusations Resulting in a Prison Sentence

During Joseph's enslavement in Egypt he earned the trust of his masters and rose in the ranks. Then, he was falsely accused of seducing his boss' wife and thrown into prison for two years as an innocent man! And yet, he remained faithful to his belief in the ultimate power of God and his understanding that he was a vessel through which God could work.

Hope: Faith in God's Power

When he was finally given a chance to use his God-given abilities to interpret Pharaoh's disturbing dreams, his life changed forever. He was put in charge of the whole kingdom and became one of the greatest administrators of all time using his organizational skills to prepare Egypt for a potentially devastating famine. His powerful position even allowed him to preserve his extended family from starvation. He had the spiritual maturity and hindsight to understand that God had used everything that had happened to him—even at the hands of others—to prepare him to be the leader for a cause much greater than himself. In the process, and unbeknownst to him, he also saved the messianic line of Judah, his brother, through whom centuries later Jesus would be born. (You'll notice that the Broadway musical missed the chance to point out that detail.)

How have you handled false accusations against you? When have you defended someone who has been falsely accused?

_____

_____

_____

_____

_____

_____

What evidence do you have that God's power can overcome difficult circumstances and help you develop necessary skills?

_____

_____

_____

_____

_____

_____

Lord, help me seek you and evidence of your power and purpose even when my circumstances seem dire.

For more of Joseph's story, read Genesis chapters 37-50.

Ruth Prepared to Help

> Boaz replied, "I've been told all about what you have done for your mother-in-law since the death of your husband—how you left your father and mother and your homeland and came to live with a people you did not know before. May the LORD repay you for what you have done. May you be richly rewarded by the LORD, the God of Israel, under whose wings you have come to take refuge."
>
> Ruth 2:11-12 NIV

Boaz noticing Ruth's character in the passage above is a good lesson for us about how God will bless us when we stand up for what is right.

Heartache: Standing Up for What is Right

It sounds strange to say that standing up for what was right would be a heartache, but I believe that doing the right thing is hard. And hard things can cause heartaches.

Ruth lived in a time when women were property, and when it was right for younger people to obey their elders. So she really broke the mold, going against customs and rules, by nearly demanding to go with her mother-in-law, Naomi, to Bethlehem. Naomi was a widow; Ruth was not only a widow but a foreigner. She risked poverty, rejection, and ridicule by doing what she did. But Ruth went anyway, knowing it was right to take care of her mother-in-law.

Once they were in Bethlehem, Naomi urged Ruth to meet Boaz, who was a family member of Naomi's deceased spouse. Ruth did everything she was told to do, and because of Ruth's outstanding character, Boaz noticed her.

Hope: Fulfillment of God's Plan

Boaz notices how important Ruth's integrity was. He noticed how she took care of Naomi and considered Ruth a woman of virtue. Eventually, Ruth won Boaz's heart and they were wed. Although none of them knew how God's plan would work out, Ruth became the mother of Obed, who was the grandfather of King David, from whose line Jesus was born.

Sometimes we can only see God's plan work out in hindsight. However, we can be assured that doing the right thing, whether its culturally accepted or not, will always lead to glorifying God. We can be confident that God has a plan both for our good and for his glory.

When was a time in your life that you risked everything to do the right thing? Were you ridiculed for it, or did someone notice and redeem it?

_____

_____

_____

_____

_____

_____

_____

_____

How can you live your life with the kind of righteousness Ruth demonstrated?

_____

_____

_____

_____

_____

_____

_____

_____

Lord, help me make decisions that add to my character, giving you glory. Show me if or how I need to go against cultural norms to serve those less fortunate.

_____

_____

_____

_____

_____

_____

_____

_____

_____

_____

_____

_____

_____

For the whole story of Ruth, read the book of Ruth in the Old Testament.

David Prepared His Heart

His advisers were amazed. "We don't understand you," they told him. "While the child was still living, you wept and refused to eat. But now that the child is dead, you have stopped your mourning and are eating again."

David replied, "I fasted and wept while the child was alive, for I said, 'Perhaps the LORD will be gracious to me and let the child live.' But why should I fast when he is dead? Can I bring him back again? I will go to him one day, but he cannot return to me."

2 Samuel 12:21-23 NLT

When you look at the life of David, you'll notice that he had many joyous triumphs, but also many heartaches. He was anointed king but couldn't take his throne for many years. He was hunted, went into hiding, and had strife in his household. Some of his trials were results of his sin, but others were because of God's plan for his life.

This account is special to me because it was the Scripture a friend's pastor read to us after our son, Andrew, died when he was 15 days old.

Heartache: When God Says "No"

I suppose, if you want to get technical, God always answers our prayers. However, he doesn't always answer them the way we want. David was fasting and praying for the life of his son. 2 Samuel 12:16-17 says:

> "David begged God to spare the child. He went without food and lay all night on the bare ground. The elders of his household pleaded with him to get up and eat with them, but he refused." (NLT)

His desperation seems palpable. David did nothing else but lay prostrate before God on the cold ground. Haven't we all been there at one time or another? Praying, pleading, begging that God will intervene?

I can relate. When we discovered our son had a serious heart defect and learned that surgery only had a slim chance of saving him, we could do little else but cry and plead to the Lord that Andrew would be okay. Like David, we got news that our son didn't survive. I didn't take this news as calmly as David did. I was a mess. I wanted to know why God didn't answer our prayers for Andrew to live.

Hope: God is Sovereign

In verses 22-33 we see that David's hope was that he would be able to see his son again in heaven. But there is more to David's response than just hoping for heaven. There was a committed belief that God is sovereign in the answers he gives us.

David accepted God's answer with grace. He got up from the cold hard floor, washed, dressed, and broke his fast. He didn't whine or complain that God wasn't fair.

He didn't demand an answer from a sovereign God who decided that a "no" was the right response to David's prayer. Instead, he trusted that God is sovereign. He knew that God is just. And he believed that God is always right.

How do you respond when God answers your prayers with a "no" or "not yet"? Are you like me, demanding answers, or like David, who accepted God's answer and returned to his responsibilities?

Lord, I confess that I don't always respond well when my prayers are not answered the way I want. Help me respond like David when you answer my prayers with a "no" or a "wait." Help me get back to my work and trust that you are sovereign over my life.

_____

_____

_____

_____

_____

_____

_____

_____

_____

_____

_____

_____

For the complete account of David losing his son, read 2 Samuel 12:15-25.

Huldah Prepared to Speak the Difficult Truth from God's Word

Hilkiah the priest, Ahikam, Akbor, Shaphan and Asaiah went to speak to the prophet Huldah, who was the wife of Shallum son of Tikvah, the son of Harhas, keeper of the wardrobe. She lived in Jerusalem, in the New Quarter. She said to them, "This is what the LORD, the God of Israel, says: Tell the man who sent you to me, 'This is what the LORD says: I am going to bring disaster on this place and its people, according to everything written in the book the king of Judah has read.'"

2 Kings 22:14-16 NIV

Wait! Who is Huldah? If you've never heard of her, you're not alone. You may know the story of King Josiah, who ordered that the Temple be restored after the previous generations had let it go to ruin. In the process, a scroll of God's law was found and brought to the king, who read it and realized he and his people had not been living up to its instructions. He sent the high priest and four other officials to the one prophet he knew could interpret the scroll accurately. That prophet was a woman named Huldah—who was never mentioned in my childhood Sunday School classes, as I recall.

Huldah's reading of the scroll would have been spiritually and emotionally painful. She would become fully aware of just how far away her people were from following God's path of proper worship, truth, and justice. She would have to deliver a dire message to the king—the difficult truth of the loss of God's favor on the people of Judah.

Heartache: The Loss of God's Favor on Her Nation

Huldah must have had the reputation of being able to discern whether or not a written document was indeed a prophetic word from God. She must have spent her life preparing for a moment like this. She probably had no idea that her knowledge of the Scriptures was going to be the key to salvation for her people. It is likely that she had not had access to the scrolls of God's Word because they were kept in the Temple, which had fallen into severe disrepair. Maybe she learned the Scriptures by memorizing what other teachers of the law had shared with her. Maybe God gave her a supernatural ability to understand the scroll the first time she saw it.

Hope: A Restored Relationship with God

Regardless of how she got the ability to explain the meaning of the scroll to the king, the end result was amazing on two counts:

1. Her interpretation helped the king realize the sins of his nation and their need to turn back to God. He called for a rededication of himself and all the people to God's Word and ways.

2. Huldah's authentication of this written document was the first step in the centuries-long process of determining which books would become the Bible we hold in our hands today. She began the canonization process of Scripture.

Huldah's appearance in Scripture is brief, but her legacy has reached us even today—we have access to her story in Scripture because she helped begin the process of preserving the books later compiled into what we call the Bible. Her ability to discern God's Word saved her nation!

What could God be preparing you to do—how can you view your gifts and skills as instruments for God's glory?

_____

_____

_____

_____

_____

What might your role be in helping to restore someone else's relationship with God or their understanding of God's Word?

_____

_____

_____

_____

_____

Lord, give me a hunger for your Word so I will be prepared to lead someone back to you with your truth.

For more of Huldah's story, read 2 Kings chapters 22-23 and 2 Chronicles chapters 34-35.

Anna Prepared to See the Long-Awaited Savior by Worshiping Daily

When the time came for the purification rites required by the Law of Moses, Joseph and Mary took him to Jerusalem to present him to the Lord (as it is written in the Law of the Lord, "Every firstborn male is to be consecrated to the Lord"), and to offer a sacrifice in keeping with what is said in the Law of the Lord: "a pair of doves or two young pigeons." Now there was a man in Jerusalem called Simeon, who was righteous and devout. He was waiting for the consolation of Israel, and the Holy Spirit was on him…There was also a prophet, Anna, the daughter of Penuel, of the tribe of Asher. She was very old; she had lived with her husband seven years after her marriage, and then was a widow until she was eighty-four. She never left the temple but worshiped night and day, fasting and praying. Coming up to them at that very moment, she gave thanks to God and spoke about the child to all who were looking forward to the redemption of Jerusalem.

Luke 2:22-25, 36-38 NIV

Spiritual disciplines can be a challenge. They demand our steadfast faithfulness even when it's difficult to fulfill the required rituals. The prophet Anna knew the discipline of daily worship. The writer of the gospel of Luke included just a few sentences about this 84-year-old widow, yet her example is one we can emulate today.

Heartache: A Lifetime of Widowhood

Widowhood in biblical times could be devastating if there were no sons to support the woman. Did Anna have children to support her? Did she have financial means from her late husband's estate? We are not given those details. What we do know is that her widowhood had not prevented her from maintaining a daily habit of worshiping her God at the Temple with prayer and fasting.

Anna's exact words are not recorded in Scripture, so she is not celebrated in song like Simeon and Mary. Yet she does hold the distinction of being the first prophet named in Scripture who saw the Christ child and then proclaimed his birth. We don't know what her previous prophecies had been and we don't know how her message was received. What we can take to heart is that her spiritual discipline of seeking God every day with prayer and fasting put her in the right place at the right time. She was there when a weary Mary and Joseph brought eight-day-old baby Jesus to the Temple to dedicate him to the Lord.

Hope: Faithful Worship Richly Rewarded

Had her prophetic gift led her to that place at that time? We don't know. But we do know that her heart was prepared to see God's long-awaited promise in the presence of a newborn infant in the arms of his faithful parents. Anna was so attuned to God's work in the world that she instantly recognized this dark-eyed, olive-skinned infant as the redemption of Israel. Can you see an elderly Anna gently cradling a squirming infant in her arms while Mary cautiously held her breath? Can you smell the scent of newborn wonder as Anna kissed his dark, fuzzy head? Can you feel the grip of those tiny fingers around Anna's sun-dried thumb?

Which daily spiritual discipline has brought you the most joy?

_____

_____

_____

_____

_____

What special touches from God or messages from God's Holy Spirit have you received in the midst of your daily habits of prayer or Bible reading?

_____

_____

_____

_____

_____

Lord, help me be so aware of your presence around me that I don't miss your long-awaited miracles.

For more of Anna's story, read Luke 2:21-40.

The Samaritan Woman Was Prepared to Discuss Deeply Troubling Questions

So [Jesus] came to a town in Samaria… Jacob's well was there, and Jesus, tired as he was from the journey, sat down by the well. It was about noon. When a Samaritan woman came to draw water, Jesus said to her, "Will you give me a drink?"…

The Samaritan woman said to him, "You are a Jew and I am a Samaritan woman. How can you ask me for a drink?" (For Jews do not associate with Samaritans.)

Jesus answered her, "If you knew the gift of God and who it is that asks you for a drink, you would have asked him and he would have given you living water"…

"Sir," the woman said, "I can see that you are a prophet. Our ancestors worshiped on this mountain, but you Jews claim that the place where we must worship is in Jerusalem."

"Woman," Jesus replied, "believe me, a time is coming when you will worship the Father neither on this mountain

> nor in Jerusalem…God is spirit, and his worshipers must worship in the Spirit and in truth."
>
> The woman said, "I know that Messiah" (called Christ) "is coming. When he comes, he will explain everything to us."
>
> Then Jesus declared, "I, the one speaking to you—I am he."
>
> John 4:5-26 NIV

Interestingly, the longest recorded theological conversation we have of Jesus talking to anyone is this one—his conversation with the Samaritan woman at the well. Maybe we should consider the deeply troubling theological issues that the woman brought up to Jesus.

Heartache: The Perceived Rejection of Her People by God

It seems to me that she had been pondering these questions for a long time and was prepared to ask them if she ever got a chance to talk to a real rabbi. These questions must have gnawed at her soul. She wanted to know if the worship the Samaritans offered to God was good enough. She was hungry and thirsty for the truth that Jesus—the promised Messiah—was offering!

Hope: Jesus, the Messiah

Have you ever finally found the answer to a question you've been asking for a long time? Maybe you're a student who finally finds the solution to a math problem, or a mom who discovers the reason your child is sick, or a teacher who comes across the perfect resource that will help your students, or a pastor who locates the Scripture passage that will communicate God's mercy to a hurting or grieving parishioner.

We all have unanswered questions deep within us. When we discover that long-awaited solution, we often find ourselves ravenously curious to learn more. That's what I sense was happening with the Samaritan woman. Finally, her heart's deepest longings were fulfilled. Those answers changed her life—and her community's life—because she invited them all into the conversation!

What questions are you asking God? Are you listening for the answer?

_____

_____

_____

_____

_____

_____

How can you share the answer you receive with others or invite them into the conversation?

_____

_____

_____

_____

_____

Lord, help me articulate my questions to you honestly with a heart ready to listen to your truth.

For more of the Samaritan woman at the well's story, read John chapter 4.

The Sick Woman Prepared for Healing

> As they went a woman who wanted to be healed came up behind and touched him, for she had been slowly bleeding for twelve years, and could find no cure (though she had spent everything she had on doctors). But the instant she touched the edge of his robe, the bleeding stopped.
>
> Luke 8:43-44 NLT

This is a beautiful story of faith and healing, but if you look a little closer, you'll see it is so much more.

According to Jewish culture and laws, this woman risked her very life: first, by being in the crowd and second, by touching Jesus. According to the book of Leviticus, a woman who was bleeding from childbirth, menstruation, or any other reason was "unclean." This meant that anything or anyone she touched would be unclean. She could not worship in the Temple, nor be near other people, because she would make them unclean as well.

Heartache: Being Sick, Ostracized, and Lonely

We can guess that the woman in this Scripture was in constant pain. She spent all she had on doctors, and still wasn't healed. She was sick, lonely, destitute, and had run out of options. She was also ostracized—for twelve years she couldn't touch anyone, not even her family. Imagine not being touched in any way for twelve years!

Knowing this helps us understand why this woman was so desperate for healing that she risked her life for a chance at hope. If she had been recognized by anyone in that crowd, she could have been put to death. Yet, her faith was so great that she thought, *If I can only touch the hem of his robe, I'll be healed!*

Hope: Jesus' Healing and Restoration

As soon as she touched the hem of Jesus' robe, he felt healing power leave him. He stopped and called her out. Surely she was scared, but she was also healed!

The Bible recounts that when the woman realized that she could not stay hidden, she began to tremble and fell to her knees in front of Jesus. Luke 8:47-48 says: "The whole crowd heard her explain why she had touched him and that she had been immediately healed. 'Daughter,' he said to her, 'your faith has made you well. Go in peace.'" (NLT)

Look at the depth of what Jesus did here. By having the woman tell her story to the crowd, he publicly restored her. She no longer had to remain alone. She publicly confessed her healing, and Jesus confirmed it—fulfilling the law that she to be declared clean before she could be welcomed back into the community. Everyone in town saw this happen, so her healing could not be denied.

This woman embraced the hope that just touching the hem of Jesus' robe would heal her, and it did. Even more than being healed, she was restored.

When have you felt ostracized or abandoned by your family or community?

_____

Jesus can bring restoration, acceptance, and belonging. How can you embrace that hope today?

_____

Lord, whenever I feel outcast or lonely, whenever I need healing from the things that take me away from community, remind me that I need to embrace hope and reach out to you in faith. For you are truly the healer and restorer of all things.

To learn more about the woman with the bleeding issue, read Luke 8:40-48.

Embrace

To embrace something means you are willing to accept or support something like a belief or a change with enthusiasm. This is why *embrace* is an important step on the journey from heartache to hope. As we reach out to God, wrestle with our questions, and have encounters that change us, we must willingly accept these changes or new beliefs. When we do, we will find healing, comfort and yes, even hope.

We pray that you will embrace what God is teaching you in the following devotionals as you journey from heartache to hope.

- Eve Embraced the Possibilities That More Children Could Bring
- Leah Embraced A God-First Attitude
- Hannah Embraced the Power of Prayer and Prophecy
- Esther Embraced God's Purpose for Her Position
- Hosea Embraced God's Redemption
- Habakkuk Embraced Joy Despite Challenging Circumstances
- Mary Embraced the Disgrace that Came with Following God's Will

- John The Baptist Embraced Jesus as Messiah
- Martha Embraced the Power of Jesus' Resurrection
- The Poor Widow Embraced Faith
- Peter Embraced Forgiveness
- John Mark Experienced Failure and Then Embraced Reconciliation
- Timothy Embraced His Calling

Eve Embraced the Possibilities That More Children Could Bring

[Eve] became pregnant and gave birth to Cain, and said, "I have given life to a man with the Lord's help." She gave birth a second time to Cain's brother Abel. Abel cared for the flocks, and Cain farmed the fertile land.

Some time later, Cain presented an offering to the Lord from the land's crops while Abel presented his flock's first offspring. The Lord looked favorably on Abel and his sacrifice but didn't look favorably on Cain and his sacrifice. Cain became very angry and looked resentful… Cain said to his brother Abel, "Let's go out to the field." When they were in the field, Cain attacked his brother Abel and killed him…

Adam knew his wife intimately again, and she gave birth to a son. She named him Seth "because God has given me another child in place of Abel, whom Cain killed."

Genesis 4:1-25 CEB

> After Seth's birth, Adam lived 800 years; he had other sons and daughters.
>
> Genesis 5:4 CEB

We have focused so much on the moment in Eve's story when the first sin was committed that we miss the rest of her story, which offers a hopeful, life-giving message. Eve was the first mother in the Bible to lose a child—and actually, she lost two children: Abel was lost to death at the hand of his brother Cain, and Cain was lost to exile. How tragic.

Heartache: The Loss of a Child

And yet…

In spite of the heartache of losing those first two children, Eve continued to have more children. We only know the name of the next son, Seth, but the Bible indicates that even more sons and daughters were born into the family over time. Hopefully, those children brought much joy and fulfillment to Eve and Adam.

Hope: Joy at the Birth of More Children

It is interesting how the Bible shows Eve—not Adam—as the only one praising God for the birth of their children (see Genesis 4:1, 25). Adam's spoken words are always focused on himself and sometimes defensive toward God and accusatory toward Eve. In Scripture, Adam never even utters God's name, while Eve does. Eve's ability to muster the desire and courage to have more children is an indicator that she trusted God's power of forgiveness and help more than she trusted her own decision-making ability. She carried with her the knowledge of her own sin, yet embraced hope and strength in God's life-giving power.

How can you prepare your heart to emerge from a tragedy in a God-honoring way?

_____

_____

_____

_____

_____

_____

_____

When have you acknowledged God's life-giving power in your own circumstances?

_____

_____

_____

_____

_____

_____

_____

Lord, help me focus on you as the source of my hope, strength, and life itself.

For more of Eve's story, read Genesis chapters 1-5.

Leah Embraced a God-First Attitude

> She conceived again, and when she gave birth to a son she said, "This time I will praise the Lord." So she named him Judah. Then she stopped having children.
> Genesis 29:35 NIV

The story of Leah and Jacob is filled with deceit and jealousy, but this time Jacob was not the cause of it. When Jacob came to his uncle's house, he saw Rachel and fell in love. His uncle, Laban, made Jacob work for seven years to win the hand of Rachel. On their wedding night, Laban veiled Leah, and Jacob consummated the marriage with her, not knowing that it was Leah instead of Rachel. Then Laban made Jacob work another seven years to wed Rachel. After Jacob and Rachel were married, there was great strife and jealousy between the sisters.

Heartache: Feeling Less-Than or Unloved

There is a lot we could talk about when we mention the heartache of Leah. She was not considered beautiful, and she may have had poor eyesight, making her a poor match as a spouse. She was not desired by anyone, and her father had to use trickery to get her married. All of these things could make a woman feel less-than or unloved—even unloveable. I think it was the contempt of Jacob that must have hurt the most. She knew that Jacob loved Rachel more, but she hoped that having sons for Jacob would make him notice her, too.

Over time, Leah bore Jacob six sons, naming them Reuben, Simeon, Levi, Judah, Issachar, Zebulun. It's interesting that the meaning of the first three sons' names were variations of "Maybe my husband will love me now." As time went on, Leah learned that her hope came only from God's love, not the validation of her husband. As a result of this growth, when she had her fourth child she named him Judah, saying, "This time I will praise the Lord." That hope in God continued: The last two sons she bore she named Issachar and Zebulun meaning, "Reward" and "Honor" respectively.

Hope: God Blesses Us When We Place Him First

It was a long road for Leah to learn how to be content and realize that the love of God was more important than anything else. When Leah embraced a God-first attitude, God blessed her in a special way for her faith: Judah, the the son she named to praise the Lord, was the line through which Jesus was born!

When we put our hope or trust in anything other than God, we will be let down. We can learn from Leah's story that people do not see beauty the way God does. Jealousy of others takes our eyes off him. And looking for validation from a spouse or partner, or even a friend, will usually let us down.

When Leah put away her self-pity and decided that her worth was in God rather than in marriage, love, or children, God blessed her obedience to him. God will never reject us when we put him first in our lives.

When you are tempted to place your value in your marriage, your children, or your work, remember the story of Leah. Only when she was content in God did he bless her abundantly.

What are the things you might be valuing more than your relationship with God?

_____

_____

_____

_____

_____

How can you become more content in your relationship with God?

_____

_____

_____

_____

_____

_____

Lord, open my eyes so I can see how much you value me. When I am tempted to put my hope in other things, or my worth in the reactions of the people around me, help me remember that I am worthy because you love me more than anyone ever could.

For more about Leah's story, read Genesis chapter 29.

Hannah Embraced the Power of Prayer and Prophecy

Because the LORD had closed Hannah's womb, her rival kept provoking her in order to irritate her… In her deep anguish Hannah prayed to the LORD, weeping bitterly. And she made a vow, saying, "LORD Almighty, if you will only look on your servant's misery and remember me, and not forget your servant but give her a son, then I will give him to the LORD for all the days of his life, and no razor will ever be used on his head"…

So in the course of time Hannah became pregnant and gave birth to a son. She named him Samuel, saying, "Because I asked the LORD for him"…After he was weaned, she took the boy with her, young as he was… and brought him to the house of the LORD at Shiloh… "So now I give him to the LORD. For his whole life he will be given over to the LORD." And he worshiped the LORD there.

1 Samuel 1:6-28 NIV

> Then Hannah prayed and said: "My heart rejoices in the LORD; in the LORD my horn is lifted high…
>
> My mouth boasts over my enemies, for I delight in your deliverance…It is not by strength that one prevails; those who oppose the LORD will be broken. The Most High will thunder from heaven; the LORD will judge the ends of the earth. He will give strength to his king and exalt the horn of his anointed."
>
> 1 Samuel 2:1, 9b-10 NIV

Heartache: The Pain of Infertility

Hannah is so relatable to anyone who has longed for a child. Nothing cuts quite so deep as the ache to love a baby of your own. Nothing stings so intensely as the taunting—real or imagined—of those who have children. Just the sight of others' children is enough to stir a flood of emotions. Hannah even had to live in the same house with the other wife who had produced multiple children for her husband, meaning Hannah was probably wife number one who had failed at producing an heir, so the husband took another wife. Oh, the agony!

However, Hannah's story doesn't end there. Hannah's example of taking her deepest heartache to God in prayer has inspired generations for centuries—the most notable being Jesus' mother, Mary, whose song of praise in Luke 1 was modeled after Hannah's prayer from 1 Samuel chapter 2. We can assume that Hannah had tried everything over the years—natural remedies and herbal treatments—in addition to prayer. Her prayers recorded in Scripture help us deduce that she was a woman of deep faith with a regular habit of talking to God.

Hope: The Power of Prayer

Hannah's prayer indicates that she believed God was capable of giving her a son. Her faith was so strong that she even made plans—before he was born (!)—to give that son over to God's service. God not only answered her specific prayer for a son, but also gave her some amazing insights into the future of her nation. Hannah embraced the power of prayer. Her prayer, recorded in 1 Samuel 2, is the first place in Scripture where the term "messiah" is used in a prophetic way (see "anointed" in v. 10). She even prophesied about the nation's king—which the nation did not yet have. Interestingly, it would be her God-given son, Samuel, who would grow up to be able to discern who would be the first two kings of Israel. Hannah's prayer life had a long-lasting influence on her son and, as a result, produced a legacy of generations of leaders.

How have your prayers for your deepest longings influenced your attitude toward those longings?

_____

_____

_____

_____

_____

_____

_____

What insights has your experience of heartache given you that you wouldn't have otherwise?

___

Lord, help me share with you my deepest longings in such a way that I will be attuned to your will like never before.

___

For more of Hannah's story, read 1 Samuel chapters 1-2.

Esther Embraced God's Purpose for Her Position

When Esther's words were reported to Mordecai, he sent back this answer: "Do not think that because you are in the king's house you alone of all the Jews will escape. For if you remain silent at this time, relief and deliverance for the Jews will arise from another place, but you and your father's family will perish. And who knows but that you have come to your royal position for such a time as this?"

Esther 4:12-14 NIV

The book of Esther is interesting because it is the only book in our Bible that doesn't specifically mention God. However, that doesn't mean than God is not present. We can learn a lot from the life of Esther, especially about how we are called to use our influence to make an impact for others rather than just ourselves. Because of God's blessings, Esther used her position in the king's household to stop a plot to kill the Jews in their land, thereby saving herself, her family, and her people.

Heartache: Being Afraid

Esther was a young girl (most scholars think she was about 14) when she was taken into the king's court. She was Jewish and very beautiful. As she gained the king's favor, God was putting her in place to do what he needed to be done. However, she was very afraid to be the only one standing up for her people.

I can understand her fears. She was was just one girl standing up for her people. She also had to deal with all of the rules and gossip and treachery of a king's household. How could a girl stand against all of that? Often her uncle, Mordecai, had to rebuke her fears, reminding her that her position gave her the ability to save God's people.

There may be times in your life when you are called to stand up for what you believe, to intervene for people, or even to admit in public that you are a Christ-follower. The thought of this may make you fearful. You might be afraid of ridicule, or conflict, or even death. These are very real fears that can be overcome by trusting God.

Hope: Trusting God

Our hope comes only in trusting God to lead us to the right place, to put us in the right position, and give us the right words to say.

Esther's trust in God and her graceful use of her position to help those in need can be an inspiration to us all. Her actions can challenge us to trust God in the circumstances in which he places us.

Maybe God is calling you to be ready for "such a time as this" to use what he has given you to help others in their time of need.

How has God blessed you by where he has placed you?

_____

_____

_____

_____

_____

_____

_____

Whom do you have compassion for that you are in a position to help?

_____

_____

_____

_____

_____

_____

_____

Lord, if you want to use me to help others, I am willing, even though I am afraid. Only show me what I can do and how I can use what you have given me to be a resource for bringing your glory and salvation to those you love.

For the whole story of Esther, read the book of Esther in the Old Testament.

Hosea Embraced God's Redemption

"Yet I will show love to the house of Judah; and I will save them—not by bow, sword or battle, or by horses and horsemen, but by the LORD their God."

Hosea 1:7 NLT

Hosea was a prophet who lived when the people of Israel strayed far from the ways of God. They worshiped idols and were unfaithful to the covenants and laws of God. God wanted to show that he is loyal and unwavering, truly steadfast in his love of his wayward people. He wanted his prophet Hosea to be an example of God's love.

Heartache: Wandering Away from God

God told Hosea to marry a woman who would be unfaithful to him the way the Israelites were being unfaithful to God. So Hosea married Gomer, a prostitute who stayed in her "profession" even after she was married.

Each time Gomer became pregnant, Hosea wasn't sure whether he was the child's father, but the Lord commanded him to claim them, so he did. Then God told Hosea to name the first child Lo-ruhama meaning,

"She has not received mercy," and the second, Lo-ammi, meaning "Not my people." These names were to show the Israelites that God condemned those who wandered away from him to worship idols.

Through all of this, Hosea was a loving and faithful husband to Gomer in the same way that God is loving and faithful to his people. even when they were sinful.

Sometimes we are like Gomer and the Israelites. We wander away from our loving God and we make foolish decisions that cause us to become enslaved. We seek our own pleasure and fulfillment, forgetting that God alone is our salvation.

Hope: Restoration and Redemption

Eventually Gomer's behavior led her into slavery, so God told Hosea to buy back her freedom. Of this, Hosea writes:

> Then the LORD said to me, "Go and love your wife again, even though she commits adultery with another lover. This will illustrate that the LORD still loves Israel, even though the people have turned to other gods and love to worship them." So I bought her back for fifteen pieces of silver and five bushels of barley and a measure of wine.
> Hosea 3:1-2 NLT

Hosea's actions show how God's love can restore even the most unfaithful. Hosea redeemed Gomer from her enslavement. God redeemed our lives through the sacrifice and blood of Jesus. John 3:16-17 says,

> "For this is how God loved the world; He gave his one and only Son, so that everyone who believes in him will not perish but

have eternal life. God sent his Son into the world not to judge the world, but to save the world through him." (NLT)

The whole Bible tells this same story. When we hide from God, he finds us. When we run away from God, he brings us back. When we are unfaithful to God, allowing our own pursuit of pleasure or passion to enslave us, God redeems us. When we don't deserve it, God saves us.

The redemption God gives is out of mercy. It isn't because we are worthy of it; it's because he loves us. It isn't because we are good; it's because he is holy.

Have you accepted the redemption of the Lord? If you haven't, pray to God accepting Jesus as your Savior. If you have, but you have strayed from his path, recommit your life to the One who loves you and saves you.

What does the redemption of the Lord look like to you?

_____

_____

_____

_____

_____

_____

_____

_____

_____

Lord, I admit I am a sinner. I have followed my own heart and my own passions, not considering what you want for my life. Today I turn away from my sin and accept your redemption for my life. I confess Jesus as my Savior and Lord, and I submit to your authority over me. Thank you for redeeming me because of your mercy and holiness. Amen.

For the whole story of the prophet Hosea, read the book of Hosea in the Old Testament.

Habakkuk Embraced Joy Despite Challenging Circumstances

> Though the fig tree does not bud
> and there are no grapes on the vines,
> though the olive crop fails
> and the fields produce no food,
> though there are no sheep in the pen
> and no cattle in the stalls,
> yet I will rejoice in the LORD,
> I will be joyful in God my Savior.
> The Sovereign LORD is my strength;
> he makes my feet like the feet of a deer,
> he enables me to tread on the heights.
> Habakkuk 3:17-19 NIV

Habakkuk is a short book in the Bible where the prophet records his questions to God, and God answers him with comfort that only he can give. Habakkuk was living in a time when evil and war raged. Tragedy befell those who believed in God, and they thought maybe he had abandoned them.

Heartache: Enduring Hard Circumstances

In a world where wrong is touted as right, and right is ridiculed and belittled, it's easy to relate to the message of Habakkuk. He goes to God with his hard questions. He writes:

> "How long, O Lord, must I call for help? But you do not listen! 'Violence is everywhere!' I cry, but you do not come to save. Must I forever see these evil deeds? Why must I watch all this misery?"
>
> Habakkuk 1:2-3a NLT

Do you feel like that sometimes? Maybe you see at all that is happening in our crazy world—conflicts, floods, famines, fires, and drought, not to mention a world full of people who are so angry they lash out at one another—and you feel distraught.

The world's anger is loud, and our circumstances are right in front of us, so they can easily distract us and make us fearful. Do you wonder where God is in all this? Like Habakkuk, do you cry out, wondering what is happening?

It can be easy to lose hope when we look at the chaos in the world. We can be tempted to think God has abandoned us just when we need him most. We can be convinced that he doesn't care what we are going through.

Like Habakkuk, we can go to God with our questions. He can handle it.

Hope: God is Still in Charge

The truth is, God *is* still with us, and he *does* care. The Bible gives us proof. We can be confident that God sees our distress (see Psalm 5:21). We can know that he will never leave us nor forsake us (see Deuteronomy 31:8).

And we can be sure that when we pray to him, he hears us. (see 1 Peter 3:12)

The third chapter of Habakkuk confirms for us that God is still in charge, and despite our circumstances, we can be joyful in him because he is our Savior and our strength.

God is good and he is in control, no matter how bad things seem around us. No matter what hardships may come our way, we can have joy and trust God.

How does knowing this give you hope in your current circumstances?

_____

_____

_____

_____

_____

_____

_____

_____

_____

_____

_____

Lord, thank you for the confidence that you are in charge of everything. You know what we are going through, and you offer us peace and joy no matter our circumstances. I will trust in your Word and let go of fear, knowing that you are in control of it all.

For more about the prophet Habakkuk, read the book of Habakkuk in the Old Testament.

Mary Embraced the Disgrace that Came with Following God's Will

> The angel answered, "The Holy Spirit will come on you, and the power of the Most High will overshadow you. So the holy one to be born will be called the Son of God...For no word from God will ever fail."
>
> "I am the Lord's servant," Mary answered. "May your word to me be fulfilled." Then the angel left her.
>
> Luke 1:35, 37-38 NIV

> This is how the birth of Jesus the Messiah came about: His mother Mary was pledged to be married to Joseph, but before they came together, she was found to be pregnant through the Holy Spirit. Because Joseph her husband was faithful to the law, and yet did not want to expose her to public disgrace, he had in mind to divorce her quietly.
>
> Matthew 1:18-19 NIV

Displays of the Nativity scene in our homes, churches, and communities never tell the whole story. The peaceful scene of a newborn's family in a stable being visited by happy shepherds and wealthy wise men is just a glimpse at a brief moment in time, and cannot convey all the events of the preceding months that led up to that starry night filled with serenading angels.

Heartache: A Ruined Reputation

Mary's decision to birth our Savior was much more complicated. Her decision meant the loss of her status as a moral young woman and a faithful bride-to-be. Her decision meant the risk of losing Joseph, the man to whom she was pledged to be married. Her decision meant the real and "legal" possibility of being stoned to death for her assumed immoral act of sex before marriage. Her decision meant she would have to endure the paralyzing heartache of rejection, false accusations, and a ruined reputation.

Mary was probably only about 14 years old, and yet her resolute faithfulness to fulfill God's will is worthy of the admiration and emulation of all ages. When she arrived at Elizabeth's house after a hurried four or five-day journey, she heard Elizabeth's comforting confirmation and the first encouragement that she was indeed blessed to be the mother of the long-awaited Messiah. When someone you love is wiling to stand with you, your endurance is so much more steadfast. Elizabeth's words to Mary reminded her—and us— that "blessed is she who has believed that the Lord would fulfill his promises to her!" (Luke 1:45 NIV)

Hope: The Knowledge of God's Choice and Purpose

The firm conviction that she was indeed following God's will, that she was fulfilling the call of God on her life, and that she was willing to die for what she believed to be true were all characteristics of the young Mary's heart. The basis of her hope—and ours—is knowing that God's purposes are worth the risking of any human reputation.

When have you known someone to risk her reputation for the greater good?

_____

_____

_____

_____

_____

_____

_____

How will your actions—based on your convictions—be remembered by future generations?

_____

_____

_____

_____

_____

_____

_____

If a moment of your life was to be displayed in paintings or on mantels, like a Nativity scene, which moment would you want it to be?

_____

_____

_____

_____

_____

_____

Lord, help me be willing to risk it all for the fulfilling of your loving purposes.

_____

_____

_____

_____

_____

_____

_____

Learn more about the life of a young Mary by reading Luke chapter 1 and Matthew chapters 1 and 2.

John The Baptist Embraced Jesus as Messiah

> The disciples of John the Baptist told John about everything Jesus was doing. So John called for two of his disciples, and he sent them to the Lord to ask him, "Are you the Messiah we've been expecting, or should we keep looking for someone else?"
> Luke 7:18-20 NLT

John the Baptist was not a man who was faint of heart. He was Jesus' cousin, the one whom God called to proclaim the Lord in the wilderness (see John 1:23, Isaiah 10:3). He baptized believers, and even Jesus himself. Yet, there was still a time that he doubted. He wondered if Jesus was really who he said he was.

Heartache: Doubting Jesus

Near the end of his life, John was in prison for speaking out against Herod. In prison, there is a lot of time to think, which can give way to doubts. Maybe John was wondering if he was really doing what he was supposed to do.

John was most likely feeling trapped and isolated. He was stuck in a situation he didn't expect, and suddenly he was questioning everything he knew to be true. Maybe you can relate.

Doubt is a tool the enemy uses to make us feel weak and unsure about our faith. It's not a new trick. If you read the Genesis story of Adam and Eve you will notice that the devil asks Eve, "Did God *really* say…?" He used doubt to lead her to disobey God.

When we doubt, we have two options. We can listen to those doubts and let our resolve weaken, or we can turn to God and ask him if what we are thinking is true. When John faced his doubts, he asked Jesus directly (well, as directly as he could). He sent his disciples to Jesus to ask, "Are you the Messiah we've been expecting, or should we keep looking for someone else?"

John's friends, and no doubt John himself, were encouraged by Jesus' answer.

Hope: Jesus is The Messiah

John's disciples found Jesus doing what he often did—healing and offering hope to the masses. They asked him John's question, and Jesus responded: "Go back to John and tell him all you have seen and heard here today: how those who were blind can see. The lame are walking without a limp. The lepers are completely healed. The deaf can hear again. The dead come back to life. And the poor are hearing the Good News. And tell him, 'Blessed is the one who does not lose his faith in me.'"
(Luke 7:22-23 TLB)

Did you notice that Jesus never condemns anyone who comes to him with questions? Instead, he answers with truth. He quoted a prophecy from Isaiah, which John would have recognized, and showed how he was fulfilling that prophecy. I'm confident that this word gave comfort to John; his life's work was not in vain! Jesus was the Messiah!

We, too, can bring our questions to Jesus when we are doubting or feeling lonely. He will never chastise or condemn us for doubting. He will answer with truth. He will show us the truth in his Word. He will help calm our uncertainty so we can carry on with the work he has given us to do.

How can you turn to Jesus in your doubt?

_____

_____

_____

_____

_____

What Scriptures is he showing you to help you calm your doubts and uncertainty?

_____

_____

_____

_____

_____

_____

Lord, I am in a season of doubt. Everything I have believed has been shaken loose, and now I'm wondering what is right. Will you please show me your truth so I can carry on with confidence and resolve?

For more about John the Baptist, read Luke chapter 3; 7:18-30, Matthew chapters 3, 9, 11, and 14.

Martha Embraced the Power of Jesus' Resurrection

"Lord," Martha said to Jesus, "if you had been here, my brother would not have died. But I know that even now God will give you whatever you ask."

Jesus said to her, "Your brother will rise again."

Martha answered, "I know he will rise again in the resurrection at the last day."

Jesus said to her, "I am the resurrection and the life. The one who believes in me will live, even though they die; and whoever lives by believing in me will never die. Do you believe this?"

"Yes, Lord," she replied, "I believe that you are the Messiah, the Son of God, who is to come into the world."

John 11:21-27 NIV

Martha is another Bible character who, in my opinion, is remembered for the wrong thing. Everyone knows the story of Martha and Mary, the two sisters who didn't see eye-to-eye on what needed to be done to feed a house full of guests (see Luke 10:38-42).

Yet, we don't often hear about the fact that it was Martha whom Jesus chose to be the first person to announce publicly his Messiahship. Interestingly, this scene takes place at a moment of deep personal tragedy: the death of her beloved brother, Lazarus.

Heartache: Death of a Close Family Member

Accompanying Martha to Lazarus' tomb, a sorrowful Jesus is surrounded by his disciples and probably some of Jerusalem's skeptical and conniving religious leaders who had followed him to see what he would do. In the conversation before he raised Lazarus from the dead, Jesus gave Martha a chance to use her voice—a woman's voice in the presence of male religious leaders who would not have accepted a woman's testimony—to announce his full divinity and her belief in the resurrection.

Hope: Resurrection Through Jesus the Messiah

Martha had fully embraced Jesus' identity as the Messiah and was willing to speak it to power. What courage! Apparently, it was more important to her to speak the truth in her heart than it was to worry about how others would respond. She spoke those words even before Lazarus was called out of his tomb by Jesus. What conviction!

When have you spoken your truth to power?

_____

_____

_____

_____

How can you express your belief in Jesus as the promised Messiah with power over death itself?

_____

_____

_____

_____

_____

_____

_____

_____

How do you explain your hope in the resurrection?

_____

_____

_____

_____

_____

_____

_____

_____

Lord, give me the words to say when I have the opportunity to speak your truth to power and in conversations about death and resurrection.

For more of Martha's story, read Luke 10:38-42; John 11:1-45 and 12:1-8.

The Poor Widow Embraced Faith

> Jesus sat down near the collection box in the Temple and watched as the crowds dropped in their money. Many rich people put in large amounts. Then a poor widow came and dropped in two small coins. Jesus called his disciples to him and said, "I tell you the truth, this poor widow has given more than all the others who are making contributions. For they gave a tiny part of their surplus, but she, poor as she is, has given everything she had to live on."
>
> Mark 12:41-44 NLT

There was nothing left. No oil. No flour. No bread. No husband to bring in more money. That was it. Two small coins. The poor widow gave it all.

Heartache: Financial Struggles

I've never been in a position where I was a widow giving my last two coins for an offering, but I can relate to this story. There was a time early in my marriage when we took a financial risk and it didn't pay off. We were truly living paycheck to paycheck. We thought that if we didn't give to our church, we would have enough money for groceries or other things we needed. Turns out, on the months we didn't give, we were out of money before the month ended, eating PB&J sandwiches for our meals.

We were convicted to give ten percent of our income (a tithe) at the beginning of each month. This wasn't much, but the strangest thing happened. At the end of the months that we gave, we always had the same amount we gave left in our bank account at the end of the month. We had our food, our bills were paid, and we had a surplus of the exact amount we gave to God at the beginning of the month.

Like the widow giving her offering, we embraced God's promises and gave in faith.

Hope: Jesus Sees Your Faith

We aren't told in the Scriptures how this story ends; we don't know if the widow was taken care of by family, or if she died begging in the streets. But here's what I do know: Jesus saw her. He knew her heart, and he saw her give everything she had to live on. He noticed. And if he noticed, God did too.

When we are obedient to what God calls us to do, he is faithful to take care of us. So, take heart. If you are struggling financially, or if you feel like you've given all you have to God in faith, you can have hope that God sees. He understands how much you have given, and he will surely take care of you.

You can be sure that God will take care of everything you need, his generosity exceeding even yours in the glory that pours from Jesus (see Philippians 4:19 MSG).

Are you living in financial insecurity? Where do you feel physically or financially "spent"?

_____

_____

_____

_____

_____

_____

_____

How have you seen God take care of your needs?

_____

_____

_____

_____

_____

_____

_____

Lord, thank you for seeing me. Thank you for understanding the enormity of my financial struggles. And thank you for taking care of all my needs.

For more about this story, read Malachi 3:10 and try giving to your church in faith.

Peter Embraced Jesus' Forgiveness

Jesus answered, "Die for me? I tell you the truth, Peter—before the rooster crows tomorrow morning, you will deny three times that you even know me.
John 13:38 NLT

So they arrested (Jesus) and led him to the high priest's home. And Peter followed at a distance. The guards lit a fire in the middle of the courtyard and sat around it, and Peter joined them there. A servant girl noticed him in the firelight and began staring at him. Finally she said, "This man was one of Jesus' followers!"

But Peter denied it. "Woman," he said, "I don't even know him!"

After a while someone else looked at him and said, "You must be one of them!"

"No, man, I'm not!" Peter retorted.

About an hour later someone else insisted, "This must be one of them, because he is a Galilean, too."

But Peter said, "Man, I don't know what you are talking about." And immediately, while he was still speaking, the rooster crowed.

At that moment the Lord turned and looked at Peter. Suddenly, the Lord's words flashed through Peter's mind: "Before the rooster crows tomorrow morning, you will deny three times that you even know me." And Peter left the courtyard, weeping bitterly.

Luke 22:54-62 NLT

Peter was a devout and enthusiastic follower of Jesus, and in the Lord's inner circle, but he was also a man led by passion and sometimes fear. He often spoke without thinking, telling Jesus earlier in this story, "Even though everyone else might abandon you, I never will!" (Luke 22:33). He was willing to risk his life and start a fight with the people arresting Jesus. But when push came to shove, when it came down to the trial, when people noticed he was a follower, he vehemently denied Jesus. As soon as he heard the rooster crow, he realized what he had done. He was so heartbroken that he ran away and wept.

Heartache: Guilt and Shame Over Denying Jesus

Perhaps you haven't publicly denied Jesus, but what about those times when we compromise on our beliefs so we don't risk ridicule? Or maybe we act out in anger, say a hurtful word, or tell a lie, and immediately feel convicted about it. There are many ways we can betray our faith, and the enemy will surely point out the times we've failed. It's part of our human condition, and Jesus understands.

Thankfully, the story of Peter continues. Peter doesn't disappear into oblivion; instead, Jesus brings him back into fellowship despite his transgression. The book of John shares an intimate conversation between Jesus and Peter when Jesus comforted the disciples after his resurrection. John 21:15-17 records Jesus asking Peter three times, "Do you really love me?" Through this conversation, Jesus allowed Peter to let go of his guilt and shame over each time he denied Jesus. Jesus restored their relationship and gave him an important mission of growing the church.

Hope: Restoration and Forgiveness

Peter was redeemed through this interaction with Jesus. As with Peter, Jesus knows that I will not live without sin or betrayal. However, I can choose to embrace Jesus' forgiveness over my failures. Like Peter, I don't have to stay in that failure.

I am comforted by this story because it shows how easily Jesus forgives. And not only that, he is ready to restore us into his work. Restoration and hope are available for those who seek forgiveness from Jesus.

How have you denied Jesus in your life?

_____

_____

_____

_____

_____

_____

_____

What can you bring to Jesus for restoration?

___

Lord, you forgive our sins so completely. And you continue to love us and allow us to serve you. Forgive me for the times I've failed, and help me see the hope and restoration you so easily give.

___

For more on the story of Peter's betrayal and restoration, read John chapter 18 and John chapter 21.

John Mark Experienced Failure and Then Embraced Reconciliation

> Some time later Paul said to Barnabas, "Let us go back and visit the believers in all the towns where we preached the word of the Lord and see how they are doing." Barnabas wanted to take John, also called Mark, with them, but Paul did not think it wise to take him, because he had deserted them in Pamphylia and had not continued with them in the work.
>
> Acts 15:36-38 NIV

John Mark, according to tradition, is thought to be the author of the gospel of Mark, which was probably the first gospel written and the source for much of Matthew's and Luke's gospels. John Mark was not one of the twelve disciples, so who was he?

Piecing together different biblical references, we learn that John Mark (known by his Roman name Mark) was a Jew, the son of another Mary, who was a wealthy widow in Jerusalem and whose home was a frequent meeting place for prayer. Peter's first letter in the New Testament seems to indicate that Mark owed his conversion to

Peter's influence. Mark's mother, Mary, was related to Barnabas (known for his encouragement), which made him Mark's uncle or cousin. Since Barnabas and Paul were close associates, Mark was brought into that inner circle of traveling missionaries. Working directly with the "encourager" Barnabas and the preacher Paul must have had a profound godly influence on Mark.

Heartache: Failure in the Eyes of a Mentor

At some point, however, Mark gave up and abandoned his missionary journeys with Barnabas and Paul. This put a wedge between Barnabas and Paul, who eventually went separate ways over this controversy. We can assume Mark felt guilt, shame, and embarrassment for causing a rift in that friendship and working relationship. Failure can feel hopeless and daunting, especially when you feel like you've let someone down whom you admire and love.

Such a tragedy can often be the sad ending of one's potential and of a relationship. However, Mark's story ends in restoration, valued service, and a legacy of gospel truth.

Paul wrote to the church in Colossae:

> "My fellow prisoner Aristarchus sends you his greetings, as does Mark, the cousin of Barnabas. (You have received instructions about him; if he comes to you, welcome him.) . . . These are the only Jews among my co-workers for the kingdom of God, and they have proved a comfort to me." (Colossians 4:10-11 NIV)

While we do not know the original reason Mark left the missionary journey with Barnabas and Paul, and we do not know what brought him back, we do know that he was restored to full favor with Paul, and became an invaluable companion and co-worker.

Hope: Forgiveness and Reconciliation

Overcoming failure is an empowering experience that is made even sweeter when it involves the gracious forgiveness of another person. These moments are a taste of God's love and mercy. When we exhibit the desire for reconnection after a broken relationship, we are being Christ-like. Jesus offers us forgiveness and reconciliation every moment of every day—all we have to do is embrace it by holding on to Jesus himself.

When have you extended the forgiveness needed to heal a rift in your relationships?

_____

_____

_____

_____

_____

What makes reconciliation so powerful after a failure?

_____

_____

_____

_____

Lord, help me extend your forgiveness to any who need to experience your grace.

For more of Mark's story, read Mark 14:51; Acts 11:24; 12:12; 13:1-5, 13:13; 15:37-38; Colossians 4:10-11; Philemon chapters 23-24; 2 Timothy 4:11; 1 Peter 5:13

Timothy Embraced His Calling

> Teach these things and insist that everyone learn them. Don't let anyone think less of you because you are young. Be an example to all believers in what you say, in the way you live, in your love, your faith, and your purity.
> 1 Timothy 4:11-12 NLT

Timothy had the arduous task of refocusing a church that let discord and false teachings divide them. In addition to taking on this leadership position in a new church, he was young, and came from a different background than the other believers.

Maybe you have felt like that: out of place as a leader, from a different heritage or cultural background, or younger than your audience. How do you deal with challenges like these?

Heartache: Being Looked Down Upon

The church at Ephesus had leaders who where preaching the Law of Moses instead of the grace of Jesus. This was dividing the church, so Paul sent Timothy to show them the Scriptures and remind them of the ways of Jesus.

It must have been such a challenge for Timothy; to be new, young, and to step up and disagree with the current leaders of the church. He was about to rock the boat in a big way!

While there is no Scripture describing how Timothy felt in his position of leadership, Paul writes him at least two letters providing encouragement and direction. Paul often told Timothy not to allow the people who were judging his age to interfere with his duty. Paul encouraged Timothy to be an example to believers by the way he lived.

Hope: Encouragement and Righteous Living

Timothy started his ministry after Jesus' death, so he didn't have a direct encounter with the Lord to give him hope. But he did receive encouragement from Paul and his family members. Encouragement from other believers is a real source of hope.

There is also hope in doing the right thing. Sometimes it's hard. Sometimes people won't understand. Paul said, "Be an example to all believers in what you say, in the way you live, in your love, your faith, and your purity." (1 Timothy 4:12) Living this way is a testimony of righteousness and truth that can't be disputed.

You can have hope that by your example, others will see the love and grace of Jesus, and learn to walk closely with him.

How do you struggle as a leader?

_____

_____

_____

_____

_____

Do you come from a different background than those you are leading? List some ways that your courage and righteous example can offer hope to those around you.

_____

_____

_____

_____

_____

_____

_____

_____

_____

Lord, thank you for the encouragement of other believers and these words of hope for young leaders who are trying to make a difference for Jesus. This brings me hope in my journey.

_____

_____

_____

_____

_____

_____

_____

_____

_____

_____

For more on the life of Timothy, read Acts chapters 16-20; 1 Corinthians 4:17 and 16:10; and the books of 1 and 2 Timothy.

On Your Way to Abundantly More Women's Retreat

With a passion for teaching women, Alane Pearce and Laura Savage-Rains have partnered to present a women's ministry event called *On Your Way to Abundantly More Retreat*. Its purpose is to help faith-filled women embrace spiritual practices on their way to celebrating joy or surviving sorrow so they can be empowered by the Holy Spirit to experience Jesus' promise of "abundantly far more."

The retreat can fit into a variety of schedules—from an hour, to a half-day event, to a full weekend retreat—with keynote speakers and small group breakouts. The event promises to be an uplifting time of fellowship, learning, and spiritual healing.

Alane and Laura will share their own private struggles with infertility, the death of a child, broken relationships, late-in-life marriage, bypassed motherhood, and painful loneliness. They will demonstrate the steps they have learned to take which always led them to truth, strength, and hope—regardless of their circumstances.

Helping women discover that they are not alone in their struggles will embolden their resolve to continue to seek the strength of the Lord.

For more information on hiring Alane and Laura
for your ministry event, please reach out to:
WomensMinistryCoach.com/contact
for pricing and details.

Alane Pearce

Alane Pearce is an author, teacher, and a coach who loves to help women see their purpose in God's plan for their lives. She spent 28 years as a military spouse, and strongly believes in the power of mentorship. She has seen many lives changed as she shares her messages of hope and encouragement to women across the country.

As an author, Alane published her own hard story: *Notes from the Margins: Healing Conversations with God,* and a companion Bible study, *Comparing Notes.* She has also been published in *Today's Christian Women, Faith and Family Magazine, 365 LifeVerse Devotional, Faith Deployed...Again, iDisciple,* and *YouVersion.*

As a speaker and teacher, Alane has led Bible studies, retreats, and seminars for women's ministry programs. Alane founded Wings for Women, a conference to help military spouses find and use the resources available to them in a post-9/11 war-focused military.

Although she looks forward to seeing eight children in heaven (seven lost by miscarriage, and one who died from a heart defect when he was 15 days old), she loves the family God created for her with her husband, Brandon, and their chosen son, Corbin.

When she is not coaching, writing, or teaching Alane enjoys a good book accompanied by strong coffee or herbal tea, depending on the time of day. She also loves cooking, traveling, and keeping up with family and friends from around the country.

Alane and Brandon, have retired to Bee Cave, Texas, and love the ambiance and the people of the hill country around Austin.

Find Alane's books on Amazon, and connect with her *@AlanePearceCoaching* on Facebook and Instagram.

Laura Savage-Rains

Laura Savage-Rains, EdD, loves to teach, speak, and write, and wishes she could do them all at the same time. As an extrovert, she much prefers the interaction of a small group of people or the energy of a big audience, but to be an award-winning author, she had to learn to sit quietly by herself with her own thoughts for hours on end. (Exhausting!)

Laura grew up in Texas as a minister's daughter and followed in her dad's footsteps by becoming a minister herself. She has worked with every age level in the local church and has trained women leaders in churches across the US. Her bachelor's degree in early childhood education (Houston Christian University) helped her to become an award-winning educator. Her seminary degree in communication (Southwestern Baptist Theological Seminary) prepared her for a variety of professional ministry roles in the local church, for being an overseas missionary, and for church lay leadership. Her doctorate in higher education administration and master's in women's studies (The University of Alabama) prepared her for teaching in universities and seminaries, leading women's groups, and coaching women leaders.

After decades of professional ministry experience, Laura is now a speaker, popular Bible teacher, women's leadership coach, and an award-winning author. She lives in Lakeway, Texas, with her long-awaited husband, Mark, who is a minister of music. Laura was 46 when they married, and was instantly blessed with three adult children: a son, a daughter, and a son-in-law, and soon, three granddaughters followed. Laura and Mark love to travel to places where they can visit art and history museums, hear beautiful music, and eat scrumptious food.

If Laura is not writing or preparing to teach, you can find her watching old movies, having coffee or lunch with girlfriends, discovering new recipes, enjoying musical events with her husband, or planning their next travel adventure.

Laura's award-winning book, *God Chose a Woman First: Discover the Keys to Resilient Confidence through the Voices of Biblical Women*, has been encouraging women of all ages to pursue God's call on their lives drawing strength from the stories of women of the Bible and their historical counterparts throughout the world. This book will remind you that God highly values women's voices, abilities, and bodies. The book explores 13 women whom God chose—instead of a man—to be the first to experience God in a new way, to express a new truth about God, or to proclaim a new message from God.

The book is available in paperback and Kindle versions on Amazon.

> Contact Laura about coaching, teaching, or speaking through her website at:
> WomensMinistryCoach.com/contact.

List of Heartaches

Page

94	A Difficult Journey Ahead with No Immediate Answers
114	A Lifetime of Widowhood
152	A Ruined Reputation
140	Being Afraid
60	Being Alone
175	Being Looked Down Upon
122	Being Sick Ostracized, and Lonely
160	Death of a Close Family Member
84	Death of a Dream—The Loss of a Loved One and All You Would Share
52	Deep Betrayal
72	Disappointment in God's Timing
68	Disapproval from Others
56	Disbelieved by Majority of Peers
155	Doubting Jesus
148	Enduring Hard Circumstances
26	Facing a Battle She Couldn't Fight Alone
46	Failed Plans and Painful Circumstances
172	Failure in the Eyes of a Mentor
98	False Accusations Resulting in a Prison Sentence
42	Family Strife in the Face of Faith
131	Feeling Less-Than or Unloved
163	Financial Struggles
38	First, Childlessness…Then, Muteness with Good News
168	Guilt and Shame Over Denying Jesus

List of Heartaches, continued

Page

- 12 Idolatry
- 34 Ignoring God
- 79 Living with a Health Issue
- 18 Loss of the Dream of the "Perfect" Family
- 64 Opposition to His Leadership
- 88 Potential Loss of Livelihood
- 30 Rejection
- 22 Running Away
- 76 Sin and Shame
- 101 Standing Up for What is Right
- 128 The Loss of a Child
- 110 The Loss of God's Favor on Her Nation
- 136 The Pain of Infertility
- 118 The Perceived Rejection of Her People by God
- 143 Wandering Away from God
- 106 When God Says "No"

List of Hopes

Page

110	A Restored Relationship with God
22	An Encounter with God
84	Birth of an Even Better Dream
77	Compassion and Forgiveness
64	Confidence in God's Call and Power
176	Encouragement and Righteous Living
72	Faith
98	Faith in God's Power
114	Faithful Worship Richly Rewarded
88	Fellowship with God's Church
173	Forgiveness and Reconciliation
52	Forgiving Restores Relationships
102	Fulfillment of God's Plan
132	God Blesses Us When We Place Him First
60	God Does Not Abandon Us
106	God is Sovereign
148	God is Still in Charge
18	God will Bless the Family You Have (Not the One You Wished for)
80	God Will Use Your Circumstances for His Glory
68	God's Plan Always Includes a Unique Role for Each of Us
46	God's Strength and Power Are Always Available
42	Jesus Gives Grace and Understanding
156	Jesus is The Messiah
164	Jesus Sees Your Faith
118	Jesus, the Messiah

List of Hopes, continued

Page

122	Jesus' Healing and Restoration
128	Joy at the Birth of More Children
26	Knowing God Would Provide Help from Others
30	Partnership with God
34	Putting God First
169	Restoration and Forgiveness
144	Restoration and Redemption
160	Resurrection Through Jesus the Messiah
56	Strength and Courage from God's Word/Law
13	The Kingdom of God
152	The Knowledge of God's Choice and Purpose
137	The Power of Prayer
140	Trusting God
39	Two Promises: Birth of a Son and Return of Voice for Prophetic Message
94	Witnessed God's Miracle at the Brink of Death

Subject Index

A

Aaron, 37, 93–94
abandon, 60, 168, 185
ability, 26, 30, 32, 110–111, 128, 140
Abraham, 17–18, 21, 23
accusations, 38, 98–99, 152, 183
adultery, 5, 11, 49, 75, 144
afraid, 37, 55, 63, 71–74, 140, 142, 183
alone, 3–4, 7, 25–26, 60, 62, 64, 84, 109, 122, 139, 144, 180, 183
Anna, 6, 91, 113–116
answers, 9, 94, 106–107, 119, 147, 156, 183

B

Barnabas, 171–172
battle, 26, 94, 143, 183
betrayal, 5, 49, 51–52, 54, 169–170, 183
birth, 17, 39, 69, 79–80, 84, 114, 127–128, 131, 135, 151–152, 185–186
bless, 18, 101, 133, 185

C

care, 60–62, 87, 102, 148, 164–166
child, 8, 17, 30, 67–68, 73, 105–106, 113–114, 118, 127–128, 132, 136, 143, 180, 184
childlessness, 8, 38, 68, 183
children, 6–8, 17–18, 51, 68, 72, 82, 114, 125, 127–128, 131, 133, 136, 179, 181, 186
church, 4, 8, 12, 51, 72, 76, 88–90, 163, 166, 169, 172, 175–176, 180–181, 185
circumstances, 4, 6, 18, 46, 62, 70, 80–82, 99–100, 125, 129, 140, 147–150, 180, 183, 185
compassion, 5, 7, 49, 75–78, 141, 185
confidence, 63–64, 73, 84, 150, 158, 182, 185
content, 132–133
courage, 56, 128, 160, 177, 186

D

David, 6, 31, 91, 102, 105–108

death, 7, 68, 72, 76, 84, 94, 96, 101, 122, 128, 140, 152, 160–162, 176, 180, 183, 186

Deborah, 5, 15, 25–26, 28

denied, 56, 122, 167–169

denying, 54, 168, 183

difficult, 6, 18, 91, 94, 99, 109–110, 114, 183

disappointment, 72, 183

disapproval, 68, 183

disbelieved, 56, 183

doubting, 155, 157, 183

dream, 18, 21, 84, 97, 183–185

E

Eli, 30

Elizabeth, 5, 37–39, 49, 67–70, 152

embrace, 4, 6, 9, 87, 123-125, 127–178

encounter, 9, 11, 18, 22–24, 39, 71–72, 91, 176, 185

encouragement, 57, 89–90, 152, 172, 176, 178–179, 185

enduring, 4, 73, 148, 183

Esau, 5, 22, 49, 51–54

Esther, 6, 125, 139–140, 142

Eve, 6, 125, 127–128, 130, 156

example, 2, 11–12, 53, 80, 114, 136, 143, 175–177

F

failed, 46, 136, 168, 170, 183

failure, 6, 126, 169, 171–173, 183

faith, 5–7, 26, 42–43, 49, 56–57, 60–62, 71–74, 98, 121–122, 124, 126, 132, 137, 156, 163–164, 166, 168, 175–176, 179–180, 183, 185

family, 8, 13, 18–19, 21, 42–44, 52–54, 60, 79–80, 88–90, 93, 98, 102, 122–123, 128, 139, 151, 160, 164, 176, 179, 183–185

favor, 67, 97, 110, 140, 173, 184

SUBJECT INDEX

fellowship, 88, 168, 180, 185

forgiveness, 6, 35, 52–54, 76–77, 98, 126, 128, 167, 169, 173–174, 185–186

forgiving, 5, 49, 51–52, 185

friends, 8, 19, 156, 179

fulfillment, 102, 128, 144, 185

G

Genesis, 17, 20–21, 24, 51, 54, 97, 100, 127–128, 130–131, 134, 156

glory, 26, 40, 79–80, 102, 104, 111, 142, 164, 185

Gomer, 143–144

good news, 38, 156, 183

grace, 40, 42–45, 48, 61, 81, 106, 174–176, 185

guilt, 63, 168–169, 172, 183

H

Habakkuk, 6, 125, 147–150

Hagar, 5, 15, 17–18, 20

Haggai, 5, 15, 33–34, 36

Hannah, 6, 30, 125, 135–138

healing, 6–7, 11, 72, 82, 91, 121–122, 124–125, 156, 179–180, 186

health, 8, 25, 79–81, 184

hear, 4–5, 9, 15, 17–48, 63, 88, 97, 156, 160

heard, 5, 15, 17–18, 21, 25, 29, 33, 37–38, 42, 45, 51–52, 63, 67, 71, 73, 75, 97, 109, 122, 152, 156, 168

help, 1–2, 5, 9, 15, 20, 25–27, 30, 32, 41–42, 44, 48–49, 54, 57, 59–61, 63, 70–71, 73–74,78, 80, 86, 90–91, 96, 99–101, 104, 108, 116, 118, 120, 127–128, 130, 134, 137–138, 140–142, 148, 154, 157, 170, 174, 179–180, 186

Herod, 37, 155

Hope, 1–7, 9, 11, 13–15, 18, 22, 26, 30, 32, 34, 39, 42–43, 46, 49, 52–53, 56–57, 59–60, 64, 68, 72–73, 77, 80, 84, 88, 91, 94–95, 98, 102, 106, 110, 114, 118, 122–125, 128–130, 132, 134, 137, 140, 144, 148–149, 152–153, 156, 160–161, 164, 169–170, 173, 176–180

189

Hosea, 6, 125, 143–144, 146

Huldah, 6, 91, 109–112

I

idolatry, 12, 184

infertility, 7, 34, 68, 136, 180, 184

Isaiah, 155–156

Israel, 23, 25–26, 29–30, 33, 101, 109, 113, 115, 137, 143–144

J

Jacob, 5, 15, 21–24, 51–52, 117, 131–132

Jairus, 5, 49, 71–74

Jesus, 5–8, 11–13, 15, 18, 41–43, 45, 49, 71–73, 75–77, 79–80, 82–85, 99, 102, 114, 117–118, 121–123, 126, 132, 136, 144–146, 151, 155–157, 159–161, 163–164, 167–170, 173, 175–176, 178, 183, 185–186

John, 6, 37, 42, 44, 75, 78–80, 82–83, 86, 118, 120, 126, 144, 155–159, 162, 167–171

John Mark, 6, 126, 171

Joseph, 5, 51, 91, 97–98, 100, 113–114, 151–152

Joshua, 5, 49, 55–56, 58

journey, 2, 9, 15, 49, 59, 91, 94, 96, 98, 117, 125, 152, 172, 178, 180, 183

joy, 5–6, 8, 18, 49, 67–70, 94, 115, 125, 128, 147, 149–150, 186

K

kingdom, 12–13, 98, 172, 186

knowing, 26, 43, 52, 102, 122, 131, 149–150, 153, 186

knowledge, 110, 128, 152, 186

L

Law, 4, 12, 56, 59, 75, 101–102, 109–110, 113, 122, 151, 175, 182, 186

Leadership, 5, 31, 64, 91, 97, 175–176, 181, 184

Leah, 6, 51, 125, 131–134

learn, 9, 21–22, 49, 65, 119, 124, 132, 139, 154,

M

Martha, 6, 41–44, 126, 159–160, 162

Mary, 5–6, 15, 41–44, 49, 67–69, 83–86, 113–115, 125, 136, 151–154, 159, 171–172

mentor, 15, 172, 183

Messiah, 6, 68–69, 118, 126, 137, 151–152, 155–157, 159–161, 185–186

miracle, 38, 68, 93–94, 186

Miriam, 5, 91, 93–94, 96

muteness, 38, 183

N

Naomi, 5, 49, 59–61, 102

Nehemiah, 5, 49, 63–64, 66

O

open, 4–5, 9, 14, 28, 49, 51–90, 134

opposition, 64, 184

others, 5, 7, 20, 23, 26, 32, 38, 46, 57–58, 60, 65, 68–70, 73, 76, 84, 89, 91, 93–94, 99, 105, 119, 132, 136, 139–140, 142, 160, 163, 176, 183, 186

P

pain, 7, 9, 18, 38, 47, 69–70, 81, 122, 136, 184

partnership, 27, 30, 186

Paul, 5, 15, 45–48, 87–90, 171–173, 175–176

peers, 56–57, 73, 183

Peter, 6, 126, 149, 167–172, 174

plan, 56, 60, 68, 102, 105, 179, 185

poor, 6, 12, 126, 131, 156, 163

possessions, 11–13, 52

possibilities, 6, 86, 125, 127

potential, 88, 172, 184

power, 5–6, 26, 31, 45–47, 49, 55–56, 63–64, 76, 79–82, 94, 98–100, 122, 125–126, 128–129, 135, 137, 151, 159–162, 179, 185–186

prayer, 5–6, 14–15, 37–39, 107, 114–115, 125, 135–137, 171, 186

prepare, 4–5, 9, 68, 91, 94–124, 129

prison, 87–88, 97–98, 155, 183

promise, 22–23, 94, 114

purpose, 5–6, 47, 49, 68, 79–80, 100, 125, 139, 152, 179, 186

Q

Questions, 6–7, 9, 91, 117–120, 125, 147–148, 156–157

R

redemption, 6, 60–61, 113, 115, 125, 143–146, 186

rejection, 30, 102, 118, 152, 184

relationships, 52–53, 88, 173, 180, 185

reputation, 13, 88, 110, 152–153, 183

restoration, 61, 122–123, 144, 169–170, 172

restored, 109–110, 122-123, 169, 173, 185

resurrection, 6, 84–85, 126, 159–162, 169, 186

reward, 132

right, 7, 12, 22, 37, 49, 53, 56, 73, 75, 101–103, 107, 114, 140, 148, 158, 176, 184

righteous, 37, 68, 76, 113, 176–177, 185

role, 68, 111, 185

ruined, 52, 152, 183

ruler, 5, 11–14

running, 11, 22, 24, 184

Ruth, 5, 59–60, 62, 91, 101–104

S

Samaritan, 6, 91, 117–120

Samuel, 5, 15, 29–32, 105–106, 108, 135–138

Scripture, 2, 8–9, 18, 34, 52, 84, 96, 105, 111, 114, 118, 122, 128, 137, 176

shame, 69, 76–77, 168–169, 172, 183–184

sick, 6, 71–72, 91, 118, 121–122, 183

sin, 38, 75–77, 79–80, 105, 128–129, 146, 169, 184

skills, 98–99, 111

sovereign, 106–108, 147, 185

spirit, 34, 45, 64, 68, 76, 113, 115, 118, 151

standing up, 101, 140, 184

strength, 8, 34, 46–48, 56–57, 60, 66, 80, 82, 129–130, 136, 147, 149, 180, 185–186

strife, 42, 51, 105, 131, 183

struggle, 7, 22, 25, 177

T

Temple, 33–34, 64, 76, 109–110, 113–114, 121, 163

temple, 33–34, 64, 76, 109–110, 113–114, 121, 163

timing, 72–73, 183

Timothy, 6, 126, 174–176, 178

trust, 3, 13, 56, 73, 98, 108, 132, 140, 149–150

trusting, 61, 73, 140, 186

U

understanding, 17, 42, 46, 98, 111, 166, 185

unloved, 131–132, 183

W

wandering, 56, 143, 184

wealth, 12–13

widow, 6, 60, 102, 113–114, 126, 163–164, 171

woman, 5–6, 17, 23, 25–26, 41, 49, 60, 67, 71–72, 75–78, 83–84, 91, 94, 96, 102, 110, 114, 117–124, 132, 137, 143, 152, 160, 167, 182

Word, 6, 9, 15, 25, 33, 42, 45, 56–58, 68, 91, 109–112, 150–151, 156–157, 168, 171, 186

worship, 5, 8, 72, 91, 93–94, 110, 114, 117–118, 121, 144, 185

Z

Zechariah, 5, 15, 37–40, 68

Scripture Index

1 Chronicles 6:3, 96
1 Corinthians 4:17, 178
1 Corinthians 16:10, 178
1 Peter 3:12, 149
1 Peter 5:13, 174
1 Samuel, book of 32
1 Samuel 1:6-28, 135
1 Samuel 1-2, 138
1 Samuel 2, 136-137
1 Samuel 2:1, 9b-10, 136
1 Samuel 3:19-20, 29
1 Timothy, book of, 178
1 Timothy 4:11-12, 175
1 Timothy 4:12, 176
2 Chronicles 34-35, 112
2 Corinthians 12, 46, 48
2 Corinthians 12:7b-10, 45-46
2 Kings 22-23, 112
2 Kings 22:14-16, 109
2 Samuel 12:15-25, 108
2 Samuel 12:16-17, 106
2 Samuel 12:21-23, 105
2 Timothy, book of, 178
2 Timothy 4:11, 174

A

Acts 9, 46
Acts 11:24, 174
Acts 12:12, 174
Acts 13:1-5, 174
Acts 13:13, 174
Acts 15:36-38, 171
Acts 15:37-38, 174
Acts 16, 90
Acts 16-20, 178
Acts 16:6-7, 45
Acts 16:14-15, 23, 25-26, 40, 87

C

Colossians 4:10-11, 172, 174

D

Deuteronomy 24:9, 96
Deuteronomy 31:8, 148

E

Esther, book of 139, 142
Esther 4:12-14, 139
Exodus 2, 96
Exodus 15, 96

Exodus 15:20-21,	93
Ezra, book of,	66
Ezra 1-5,	36

G

Genesis 1-5,	130
Genesis 4:1-25,	127
Genesis 4:1, 25	128
Genesis 5:4,	128
Genesis 16:1-15,	20
Genesis 16:9, 11,	17
Genesis 21:8-21,	20
Genesis 25-50,	24
Genesis 25:12-18,	20
Genesis 27, 32, 33,	54
Genesis 28:11-15,	21
Genesis 29,	134
Genesis 29:35,	131
Genesis 33:1-4,	51
Genesis 39:20-21; 41:1-40,	97

H

Habakkuk, book of	150
Habakkuk 1:2-3a,	148
Habakkuk 3:17-19,	147
Haggai, book of	33-34, 36
Haggai 1:3-6,	33
Hosea, book of	146
Hosea 1:7,	143
Hosea 3:1-2,	144

I

Isaiah 10:3,	155

J

John, book of,	168
John 1:23,	155
John 3:16-17,	144-145
John 4,	120
John 4:5-26,	117-118
John 7:53-8:11,	78
John 8:3-11,	75
John 9:1-3,	79
John 9:3,	82
John 9:32-33,	80
John 11,	44
John 11:1-45,	162
John 11:21-27,	159
John 12:1-3,	42
John 12:1-8,	162
John 13:38,	167
John 18,	170
John 19-20,	86
John 20:14-17,	83
John 21,	170
John 21:15-17,	169

Joshua, book of	58
Joshua 1:5-7,	56
Judges 4-5,	28
Judges 4:6-9,	25

L

Luke 1,	40, 70, 136, 154
Luke 1:5-7, 11-13, 18-20,	37-38
Luke 1:6,	68
Luke 1:25, 36-37, 39, 42-45,	67
Luke 1:35, 37-38,	151
Luke 1:45	152
Luke 2:21-40,	116
Luke 2:22-25, 36-38,	113
Luke 3,	158
Luke 7:18-20,	155
Luke 7:18-30,	158
Luke 7:22-23,	156
Luke 8,	86
Luke 8:1-3,	84
Luke 8:43-44,	121
Luke 8:47-48,	122
Luke 8:40-48,	124
Luke 10,	44
Luke 10:38-42,	41, 159, 162
Luke 18:18-30,	14
Luke 22:33,	168
Luke 22:54-62,	167-168
Luke 24,	86

M

Malachi 3:10,	166
Mark 5:22-24,	35-36, 71
Mark 5:22-43,	74
Mark 5:36,	72
Mark 5:37,	72
Mark 5:39-40,	72
Mark 10:17-22,	11-12
Mark 10:17-31,	14
Mark 12:41-44,	163
Mark 14:51,	174
Mark 15-16,	86
Matthew 1-2,	154
Matthew 1:18-19	151
Matthew 3,	158
Matthew 9,	158
Matthew 11,	158
Matthew 14,	158
Matthew 27-28,	86
Micah 6:4,	96

N

Nehemiah, book of	66
Nehemiah 4:1, 4-6,	63
Nehemiah 6:16,	63

Numbers 12, 96
Numbers 14:6-10a, 55
Numbers 20, 96
Numbers 26, 96

P

Philemon 23-24, 174
Philippians, letter to the 90
Philippians 4:19, 164
Psalm 5:21 148
Psalm 62:1-2, 5-8, 3

R

Romans 3:10, 76
Ruth, book of 62, 104
Ruth 1:7-9, 59
Ruth 2:11-12, 101

Acknowledgments

First of all, we would like to thank the Lord for his saving grace and love, and for the gift of writing and creativity that he has bestowed upon us.

We are grateful for the blessings of a fun writing friendship—a rare gift to be of the same mind so often!

We are thankful for our husbands, Brandon and Mark, for patiently enduring our long afternoons (and evenings) of writing, editing, proofing, and birthing this book.

We have found a rare gem in Sheryl Disher, an amazing editor who understood the ministry purpose of this work. Thank you!

Made in United States
Troutdale, OR
09/26/2024

23146217R00116